Integrity in Business

Integrity in Business

Developing Ethical Behavior Across Cultures and Jurisdictions

FRANK HOLDER

Routledge
Taylor & Francis Group

LONDON AND NEW YORK

First published 2013 by Gower Publishing

Published 2016 by Routledge
2 Park Square, Milton Park, Abingdon, Oxon OX14 4RN
711 Third Avenue, New York, NY 10017, USA

Routledge is an imprint of the Taylor & Francis Group, an informa business

British Library Cataloguing in Publication Data
Holder, Frank.
  Integrity in business : developing ethical behavior across
  cultures and jurisdictions.
  1. Business ethics. 2. International business enterprises--
  Management.
  I. Title
  174.4-dc23

The Library of Congress has catalogued the printed edition as follows:
Holder, Frank.
  Integrity in business : developing ethical behavior across cultures and jurisdictions / by
  Frank Holder.
      p. cm.
  Includes bibliographical references and index.
  ISBN 978-0-566-09187-2 (hbk.) -- ISBN 978-1-4094-5766-4 (ebook)
  1. Business ethics. 2. Corporations--Moral and ethical aspects. 3. Fraud. I. Title.
  HF5387.H654 2013
  174'.4--dc23

                                                                    2012035588

ISBN 13: 978-0-566-09187-2 (hbk)

CONTENTS

LIST OF FIGURES

LIST OF TABLES

ABOUT THE AUTHOR

Frank L. Holder is Chairman of the Latin American region of FTI Consulting, which includes offices in Buenos Aires, Bogotá, Mexico City, Panama City, São Paulo and Rio de Janeiro. Based in the regional headquarters in Miami, Dr. Holder has been leader of the Forensic and Litigation Consulting practice in Latin America since 2007.

Dr. Holder has directed corporate investigations and security consulting assignments in Latin America and the United States. The investigative matters include large-scale internal fraud and public corruption investigations, product protection, litigation support, due diligence and hostile takeovers. As a security expert, he has designed the security for international airports, seaports and complex multi-jurisdictional distribution networks.

Dr. Holder is fluent in English, Spanish and Portuguese. He is an accomplished public speaker with numerous presentations throughout the United States, the UK, Argentina, Chile, Mexico and Brazil on a broad range of topics such as money laundering, risk management, homeland security and operational risk. He has written articles on similar topics for US and Latin American newspapers and professional journals. He has taught courses in political science and law on the Inter-American system at the Universidad del Salvador, Buenos Aires. He is the author of *Narcotics Trafficking: A Constructed Typology of the Deviant Market of Illicit Drugs*.

Dr. Holder was the chief executive officer of Holder International, which was acquired by FTI Consulting in 2007. Prior to founding Holder International, he was the president of Kroll, Inc.'s Consulting Services Group, responsible for operations in more than 35 countries around the world. Prior to that, he was the head of Kroll's Latin America and Caribbean region. Before joining Kroll, he was the president of Holder Associates in Buenos Aires, a risk mitigation and business intelligence firm.

Dr. Holder began his career with the US Air Force as a political-military analyst for the US embassy in Argentina and as a special agent for the Office of Special

Investigations at Langley Air Force Base in Virginia, with responsibilities in the counter-intelligence and force protection areas, among others.

Dr. Holder holds a PhD and an MA in political science from the Universidad de Belgrano in Argentina and is a summa cum laude graduate of the US Air Force Academy. He won the Airman's Medal for valour for his actions in the aftermath of the AMIA bombing in Buenos Aires.

For more information about Frank Holder, please visit www.frankholder.com.

CHAPTER ONE

THE MYTH OF AMORAL BUSINESS

There are a multitude of books, articles and white papers written on the subject of business ethics. Some involve case studies or tell a history of ethics in business, while others focus on a religious and/or personal moral theme. This book will answer the question 'What is business ethics?' and provide a guide on how you can improve your business ethics. There are far fewer references on business integrity promoting the value of integrity as a strategy and a prerequisite for successful business in a globalized world. There are also a number of titles written in textbook or academic styles. Consequently, there are few books that are written as practical guides for professional practitioners who have to struggle with business integrity issues as they relate to their everyday businesses. The assertion, by the more cynical commentators, that business and integrity are contradictory and oxymoronic dismisses further examination into the evolution of best practices, serves as an effortless explanation about why some organizations have failed, and plainly ignores the trend towards more compliance in a globalized world. It is very simple: integrity in business today is not only about decisions willingly made by organizations, but also the individuals employed by the organization, its key partners and suppliers, clients and market trends. The requirement to comply with rules and regulations is growing and the trend towards more transparency *requires* individuals and organizations to perform their appointed tasks with the highest level of integrity or risk damaging their reputation and the reputations of their associates and/or clients. This book will discuss the trend towards more transparency and how cases of fraud and corruption are increasingly being exposed. Fraud and corruption by individuals and businesses is now in the spotlight, especially because of the ability of the media to have an aggressive and exponential effect on public awareness and perception. The result of this awareness is twofold. First, media technology is helping regulators keep fraud a salient issue with each new discovery and helping grow the public's demand for officials legislate against fraud. It has indeed become a hot-button issue, especially after the downturn of the global economy. Second, this awareness is causing us to ask questions about how much legislation is needed to prevent fraud while allowing businesses to remain competitive in the global market. The increase in fraud and corruption, legislation in response to it and rise in awareness due to media technology has produced a dilemma. Fraud needs to be curtailed and transparency is key to any solution, but there are limitations that come with too much regulation for businesses. It is not necessary to lose a competitive edge in the marketplace to ensure integrity. In fact, there are ways that businesses can work with governments, utilize the guidelines set by non-governmental organizations and their experts to combat corruption, and police themselves to ensure they function with integrity.

This book aims to focus, at times, on the complex nature of integrity and business and to demonstrate how organizations have avoided major setbacks to their reputations and market value by encouraging integrity. These same organizations have avoided setbacks because they identify and manage strategically those organizations with whom they transacted business; by using competitive intelligence, followed by diligent relationship management, they have exercised proper due diligence. The examples used will demonstrate how the more successful organizations also happen to be the most transparent, have top-down approaches to fostering integrity and—most importantly—have strategies to identify, manage and avoid organizations and/or individuals that pose a risk to their reputations. We will also examine those organizations that have failed and/or experienced reputational damage due to a lack of preparation; lack of transparency, lack of the kind of leadership which facilitates an environment where integrity is key, and failure to exercise due diligence when doing business. We will explore the lessons of these failed organizations in order to identify what went wrong and to develop a practical guide either to fix or prevent similar issues in your own organization with the hope that you will be armed with strategies—based on a set of tools learned through these examples—of how other organizations have prevented a crisis, or completely recovered following a major issue. This practical guide will ensure continuity in the event of a potential public relations crisis surrounding your business ethics and includes perspectives on how to measure your business integrity and take action in a globalized business environment.

One unavoidable trend in the past 50 years has been the development of technologies that are making the world increasingly interconnected. These technologies range from communication to transportation and have revolutionized the way the world works and how we perceive it. These technologies inevitably caused changes in business as well. These changes, which are global in nature, are central to each argument in this book. They reflect the new difficulties that have been produced in businesses and what organizations are doing to deal with them. For practitioners concerned with the difficulties of running multi-jurisdictional and multicultural organizations in today's complex compliance environment, insight into how this trend has changed the rules of the game is critical. I have written this practical guide for c-suite officers, directors of companies, general counsels, audit departments, compliance officers, government agencies and professional services firms in the legal, audit, tax and consulting areas. I have included both a case study methodology, using only the most germane and up-to-date cases, as well as a comparative analysis of the current regulatory environment in the world, while looking at a brief history of the evolution of integrity and business, drivers of current behavior, and an analysis of what is wrong as well as practical tips in the final two chapters on how to fix it. All of these practical tips will serve to provide a guideline for doing business in a globalizing world.

The interconnections driven by globalization cannot be perceived as a process that standardizes the global business environment. 'Globalization' must be understood as a complex set of interacting processes and not a standard homogenized process. The word is more aspirational than real and in the gaps between the concept and the reality lie significant risks. Therefore, this practical guide exposes the trends of globalization across different markets, specifically in Chapters 2 and 3, and highlights the value of being informed about every aspect of your business and the global market, and examines the risks to your business integrity when you or your organization only concentrate on your proximate concerns without examining the risks posed by your key partners and suppliers and clients during your due diligence efforts. As Chapter 4 highlights, fraud and corruption could have been prevented if a few individuals, whether internally or externally, took additional steps and scrutinized the individuals and/or companies they were conducting business with and brought attention to any inconsistencies like unusually high returns in a bear market in the case of Bernard L. Madoff's Ponzi scheme. Fortunately, these additional steps are not costly. Access to information today is more available due to more stringent legislation mandating transparency, worldwide awareness of corruption and media technology. Information is a critical asset and must therefore be protected while conduct must be as transparent and clear as possible. There is no room in today's world for grey and/or mixed messages because the penalties and risks are too high. This holistic approach ensures your information remains up-to-date and relevant and provides preparedness while simultaneously safeguarding conduct, guaranteeing business integrity, and confirming a great reputation.

It is not an easy task to set forth an argument on how integrity can successfully be present in companies without compromising revenue because a company could never be fully transparent. In fact, it is important that companies have trade secret protections and penalties for disclosure of proprietary information by employees who signed non-disclosure, or who have non-compete clauses in their contracts, act as disincentives. At the heart of every successful business there is a special formula, process, design, and/or information that allows for a legal competitive advantage in the marketplace. This can be done without compromising integrity. Competition remains at the heart of business and entrepreneurship. This will not change. It may seem as if there is no integrity due to the privileged nature of information, but this is the foundation of a fair market system: you have an innovative idea, you protect that idea, your idea becomes obsolete as a result of improvements or disinterest, and a new idea arises. The speed of business creates a circumstance in which today's groundbreaking idea is tomorrow's outmoded and largely forgotten commodity. Whether these ideas drive, or are driven by technological advances, rapid changes in the way we do business are inevitable. Such changes force leadership in organizations to be more cognizant and knowledgeable about the reputations of their associates and cautious about the risks posed by conducting business with another organization and/or individual that possesses a questionable background. Transparency, whether through self-policing or mandated through legislation, does not mean that a company has to provide access to its 'secret sauce' and, in turn, its trade secret protection. Instead, it simply means that there needs to be a fair balance in competition, and knowing whom you are doing business with is essential to ensuring your company is protecting itself from internal and external corruption while maintaining a positive reputation in the open market. To protect itself and customers, every company should take a holistic layered integrity/business ethics approach to achieving this balance (see Figure 1.1). Most importantly, while the scope of leadership's awareness is now global, establishing integrity within local markets still remains the foundation of any business. The integration of market systems, coupled with the upsurge of social media, makes it so that it is no longer sufficient to remain concerned with your immediate surroundings (i.e., you, your organization, clients, key partners and suppliers) at any given time. The greatest lesson learned from failed companies, those that recovered successfully from a crisis, or those that have proved remarkably resilient and never suffered a public relations predicament was the value of being informed. Those who were able to remain in business were more likely to have had more understanding about its immediate dealings as well as thorough information about their clients and the market at any given time. They were prepared. Unfortunately, some were not prepared or were 'wilfully blind' to corruption and no longer exist. In addition, the corruption in failed companies such as Enron, WorldCom and Bernard L. Madoff Investment Securities LLC have led to widespread collateral damage and have caused other companies to fail (e.g., Arthur Andersen (Enron)), milked investors of their funds, and caused employees their pensions and jobs. Furthermore, it has led to lost confidence in the market.

The consequences of not knowing and understanding the organizations and/or individuals with whom you are doing business were considered insignificant for companies in the past because it seemed the risks were low, but this is no longer the case. We are increasingly interconnected and the value of your reputation is now combined with severe penalties for non-compliance. The US Foreign Corrupt Practices Act of 1977 (FCPA), which is discussed in Chapter 5, along with other drivers of current behavior, serves as an example of the importance of knowing your customers and your suppliers prior to engaging in any business dealings with them. In fact, the FCPA was amended in 1998 and was considered the strongest legislation in the fight against corruption until the United Kingdom's Bribery Act of 2010. Both the US FCPA's 1998 amendment and UK Bribery Act of 2010 serve as examples of governments' responses to corruption. However, while governments across the globe are affording their respective regulatory agencies

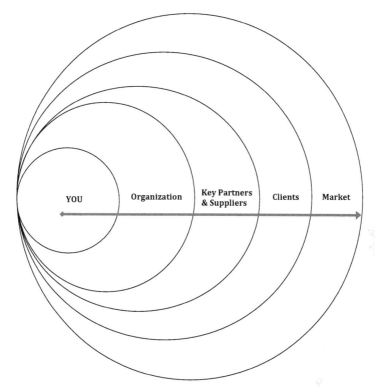

Figure 1.1   **Holistic layered integrity/business ethics approach**

more resources and introducing legislation to combat corruption in order to ensure investor confidence and business integrity, companies must also be responsible for the enforcement of their internal compliance systems as well. These compliance systems must be able to adjust to governmental changes, company policies and personnel. Otherwise, the system itself risks becoming rigid and/or obsolete. A company's compliance system must be enforced as strongly as legislation mandates. It needs to be internally enforced as well and, in order to be effective and ensure key partners and suppliers, clients and employees in your company do not act with poor judgement, these acts of indiscretion should be dealt with accordingly. Governments and companies will have different understandings about what constitutes corruption. However, having company compliance guidelines, awareness of them, and enforcing them will provide clarity to your values.

What constitutes integrity in business has *evolved* just as many other values-based concepts have. It was as recently as 2000 that the French government started to identify the differences between passive and active bribery and imposed an international treaty regarding the payment of bribes in commercial contracts. Officially known as 'exceptional commercial expenses', these bribes were acceptable.[1] Today, they are largely unacceptable and are discouraged with sanctions and penalties. Value-based concepts have changed in no little part because business increasingly crosses international boundaries and new cultures; e.g., the Chinese, the Indians and the Brazilians are starting to influence the way the world conducts its business. Technology and transparency are making it more difficult to conceal bribes and/or deny them when they do happen—the same transparency is true with incentives offered for exceptional performance. In addition, transnational regulatory organizations such Transparency International (TI), the Organisation for Economic Cooperation and Development (OECD), and Partnering Against Corruption Initiative (PACI) are spearheading the movement to ensure bribery in international business is monitored and criminalized. Later in the book, I will discuss the significance of these non-governmental regulatory organizations and government actions as well as their ability to prevent corruption and encourage transparency and integrity. Prior to discussing these organizations and governmental legislation thoroughly, we have to have a better understanding of fraud, the motive, the method and the people and/or companies that committed fraud. Companies have to be aware of the motives and methods fraudsters used to cover their schemes and how their own corporate structure and way of conducting business can allow for fraud and corruption within its rank. Companies need to adopt standards and create a culture that emphasizes anti-corruption. A company's internal compliance policies are the foundation upon which everything else is built.

DEFINING BUSINESS

The seminal examples of corruption and lack of transparency in businesses in the first decade of the twenty-first century are Enron's accounting fraud discovered in 2001, the HP spying scandal in 2006, Siemen AG's corruption and bribery scandal discovered in 2008, and several Ponzi schemes carried out, specifically Bernard L. Madoff's scheme, to name a few. It is not a surprise that the public, with the aid of the media, are demanding fundamental change in the way companies conduct business. Of course, it is important to get a sense of perspective. The majority of business transactions are honest and compliant, but the fraudulent anomalies are what make headlines in the media. This is especially true when hindsight provides us with various gaffes by regulatory agencies that could have stopped or, at the very least, prevented these fraudulent activities from getting worse. This is

---

1   Organisation of Economic Co-Operation and Development. Directorate for Financial, Fiscal, and Enterprise Affairs. *France: Phase 2. Report on the Application of the Convention on Combating Bribery of Foreign Public Officials in International Business Transactions and the 1997 Recommendation on Combating Bribery in International Business Transactions.* Working Group on Bribery in International Business Transactions (CIME). 22 January 2004.

why companies must have the tools to police themselves and minimize risks and liabilities. The fact is that, while regulatory agencies may hurt their reputations for failing to notice fraud, your company will be penalized and probably fold. While businesses have a more difficult time regaining their image and reputations, regulatory agencies are able to quickly change administrative leadership and continue to rebuild after a public relations disaster. Companies do not have the benefit of starting over. Thus, it is more imperative for companies to establish internal controls on their own along with governmental mandates. This will minimize your company's risks and liabilities and serve as a preventative tool to deter fraud.

Unfortunately, fraudulent activity within one part of a business or one industry is extraordinarily corrosive and infectious to those around it. Thus, the scandal that engulfed Enron not only affected Enron and its subsidiaries also led to the collapse of other firms, such as the accounting firm of Arthur Andersen, associated with Enron. Therefore, if your company is connected with a lack of integrity, even if that connection is by association with a third party, it becomes a risk even if you are fully compliant and the culture of your company thrives on integrity. While your company may have procedures and resources to establish a strong internal compliance system that adheres to legislative mandates, the companies and individuals you conduct business may lack them. Your compliance system must include a set of procedures that must be satisfied prior to conducting business; this will be discussed in Chapters 6 and 7 where I discuss optimal solutions regarding fraud and corruption prevention. However, it must be noted that integrity is a value-based concept. It is difficult and, at times, impossible to fully define a value-based concept like integrity, let alone in a company that does business across multi-jurisdictional and multicultural settings. We have to look at the consistency of actions of a company and its employees and how they resolve any inconsistencies they face. A company's culture, and value systems within that culture, go a long way to determining whether or not it has the ability to prevent corruption as well as survive it. In my experience, the following is a summary of how companies can measure their integrity.

The Measure of Integrity

How do we measure a company's integrity and validate that its employees will act responsibly, especially when placed in a difficult position? Increased rules, greater competition and access to new, more geographically disparate markets have increased the risk of dubious business practice, without necessarily defining the picture of what this actually means in practice. Business integrity requires us to examine, among other things, organizational behavior (i.e., its culture of compliance), how the company is structured, details about the company's associations and clients, whether it facilitates an open platform for discussion, how compliance issues are dealt with and whether transparency exists. The following are potential key measures by which you can assess the level of integrity within your company:

1. Policies, vision and mission
2. Tone from the top and leadership
3. Training and awareness
4. Consequences (including, penalties and termination for poor judgement)
5. Whistle-blower and similar internal control programs.

An effective company implements policies that provide a structure to the workplace. The process of measuring integrity and how it functions in a globalized business world begins with a glance at a company's policies and whether or not these policies are understood by employees. While a company's vision and mission may be answered in simple, and often creative, statements, a company's policies are what drive behavior. In addition to policies, a vision and a clear mission, these procedures must be supplemented with training, awareness of the consequences of not following these procedures, and whistle-blower and other internal control programs. Most importantly, leadership is directly responsible for ensuring employees are not only aware of the above measures of integrity, but also set the tone and transparently perform their duties by example. These measures of integrity will be discussed throughout this guide to ascertain the positive and negative lessons learned. Throughout my examination of fraud and corruption cases, I found that fraudulent activities were committed when one or more of these measures of integrity were lacking. Ensuring these above measures are examined and positively enforced will offer your company the inexorable effect of transparency as the broader tool to combat corruption.

Transparency: Does It Exist in Your Company?

Transparency represents two ideals in a company. The first will be discussed in relation to compliance programs that require companies and their employees to disclose material matters relating to the business process in a timely and balanced manner to ensure all investors, stakeholders and relevant authorities have unobstructed access to relevant information about the company. This understanding of transparency also informs investors, stakeholders and relevant authorities about the roles and responsibilities of key management in the company in order to assess accountability. It is generally accepted that companies minimize their risk of violating legalities by creating greater transparency. Thus, this ideal of transparency in a company is concerned with mitigating risks and preventing lawsuits. It also applies to codes of conduct that your company, its directors and executives and employees must adhere to when doing business. More importantly, leadership (i.e., senior management) in these companies is required to implement procedures that uphold the integrity of the entire company's financial reporting, decision-making responsibilities and provide shareholders and authorities access to this information, especially if it is mandated by legislation.

The second ideal of transparency in a company is one that is not controlled by compliance programs at all. Aside from relying on regulatory agencies through legislation to require companies to disclose relevant material matters in a timely manner, there are also reputational standards that are increasingly becoming just as important in a globalized world. A routine online search on your company will provide your potential partners, suppliers and clients the opportunity to know your reputation, even if it is on a superficial level. Your online reputation impacts your company. Business today does not function in a vacuum. Instead, companies and their business dealings are also bound by media pressures to be transparent to some degree. Trade secrets and intellectual property are still very much protected today and this book does not argue for radical transparency. These are what create competition in a fair market system that works. Transparency comes in two ideals within a company: forced and unforced. That is, on the one hand, companies face the pressures of authorities and compliance programs that are concerned with specific reporting standards while, on the other hand, the media pressure exists because the audience is now global and ethical and responsible decision-making from a public relations standpoint is equally important. In any case, a company's level of transparency is increasingly linked to its perceived integrity in an interconnected world with advanced media technologies.

What is Globalization?

Globalization is framed around the basic suggestion that it involves the flawless integration of nation-states and that it is creating a bridge between previously disconnected people, governmental/non-governmental institutions, markets and ideas. On the contrary, a globalized world does not mean one where interconnections naturally create interdependence, transparency and integrity. This type of thinking is limiting and is not how globalization works; the 'invisible hand' will not do the work for you. A globalized world is a more competitive world and organizations and companies that succeed have an open platform for innovators, a great understanding of their products, services and associations, and have a strong interest in ensuring they are in compliance. As Thomas Friedman states, in a globalized world, market forces will continue to work on the idea that '[n] othing matters so much as what will come next, and what will come next can only arrive if what is here now gets overturned'.[2] We have already discussed the terms 'business' and 'integrity', including how exercising due diligence, transparency and providing an open platform in your organization results in optimal success. In order to understand how the value of these terms in today's market and how

---

2   Thomas Friedman. *The World is Flat: A Brief History of the Twenty-First Century.* Farrar, Straus and Giroux. 2005.

their meanings have evolved to form a nexus and inexorable relationship, we have to examine the process of globalization as it relates to the changes in the market environment: that is, the interconnectedness globalization has created among governmental and non-governmental organizations and companies across markets has augmented the importance of time—in terms of how quickly an idea becomes obsolete as well as how quickly that idea travels. Companies have to evolve and adapt to the changes globalization has caused and quickly adjust, internally and externally, to newer control systems.

Let us imagine a factory during the Industrial Revolution. Mass production during the period initiated the process of production to be repetitive, consistent and precise. It also required order in the form of rules, order in the form of the workers' specific tasks, and order in the form of the factory's floor plan. This was necessary to ensure the factory produced the supply that equaled the demand. Therefore, the factory system required order in the form of full compliance of regulations, project management/time-on-task and a platform that was conducive to getting it done right the first time. Now, let us imagine a company today. The term 'globalization' has become a celebrated buzzword for the changes we have experienced in the past 50 years and, more intensely, in the past 20 years. Globalization and global processes have to be defined in order to demonstrate how the increase in transparency coupled with the growth of multicultural and multi-jurisdictional businesses have directly and positively affected the evolution of integrity and business. As I mentioned above, a global business environment requires you to focus on all aspects that may impact your business. This holistic approach to business ethics will require you to focus on fraud, and how it is policed, outside your market: is it illegal, sanctioned, accepted practice, or simply frowned upon? What I found over the course of my business career and owning multinational companies is that countries with the weakest compliance systems usually have had lesser assets allocated to them to oversee wrongdoings, whereas countries with strong compliance systems have greater assets than necessary which often creates a congested bureaucracy. In fact I will show how, in several high-profile cases across the globe, having too many assets allocated within a strong compliance system created a bottleneck and actually slowed the discovery of fraud. Firms must allocate more resources to areas where the actual risks are likely to exist, such as emerging rather than developed or home markets (see Figure 1.2, Assets are allocated to integrity asymmetrically). Figure 1.2 provides a simple illustration of how lower risk developed or home markets are adequately (and even abundantly) prepared with compliance officers, whereas higher risk developing markets are not armed with the assets necessary to ensure full compliance and operate with minimal risks.

In Chapter 6, I will discuss how the optimal solution is asset reallocation. The initial step to protecting your company via asset reallocation is similar to the initial steps of a business continuity/crisis management plan. That is, you dissect your

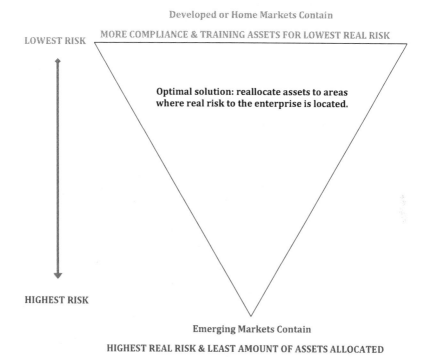

INTEGRITY IS A GLOBAL ISSUE IN TODAY'S BUSINESS ENVIRONMENT

Developed or Home Markets Contain

LOWEST RISK   MORE COMPLIANCE & TRAINING ASSETS FOR LOWEST REAL RISK

Optimal solution: reallocate assets to areas where real risk to the enterprise is located.

HIGHEST RISK

Emerging Markets Contain

HIGHEST REAL RISK & LEAST AMOUNT OF ASSETS ALLOCATED

Figure 1.2   Assets are allocated to integrity asymmetrically

company, analyze the functions of each department and/or location and ensure there is a direct line to compliance as well as accountability.

During the boom of the Industrial Revolution, the process of production was stratified. The boss understood the industry, understood the process of production, and trained and managed the workers for specific tasks. The Industrial Revolution yielded businesses that required workers to be repetitive and the boss had to be entrepreneurial. The system of production created during the Industrial Revolution and the economic circumstances of the times led to backroom deals, closed-office meetings and a highly stratified workforce. It is simple to ascertain why the idea of integrity in business is written off as an oxymoron by just comparing the knowledge gap this system created between the boss and worker as well as the overall lack of transparency. Integrity is not a virtue that was commonly thought about with regards to the factory system, at least not until unions were created. It is nearly impossible to have full confidence in businesses without transparency and a highly stratified workforce. A globalized world has also caused stratifications and will continue to do so as it transforms and continues to change the way we do business. Like the Industrial Revolution in the past, globalization today is but the latest stage in a long accumulation of technological advancements and changes in societal thought that has given human beings the ability to conduct their affairs across the world. Globalization is precisely the interdependent need for people, nations and markets to create goods and services that can be used across the board and the will to work together. This move towards interdependence requires rules and enforcement. Today, we are witnessing (and, often demanding) the growth of regulatory governmental and non-governmental organizations at every level, from local to national, that monitor businesses and ensure they are operating under the law of their respective compliance system. A standard is being created.

The evolution of integrity and business entails painting a brief picture of how businesses evolved from one stage of intense changes and development to the next and how these changes not only affect how organizations function but also how we have reacted to these chaotic conditions by setting rules and regulations. The United States Securities Exchange Commission (SEC) was created as a result of the stock market crash of 1929 that gave way to the Great Depression. The US SEC enforces, among other Acts, the United States Securities Act of 1933, and the Sarbanes–Oxley Act of 2002 exposed large corporate frauds between the years 2000 and 2002. It is not a surprise that each of these Acts was created to either fix chaotic and vague business systems or to expose them; interestingly, our research finds that the increase in compliance programs and transparency has led to more integrity in business. The United States Patriot Act of 2001 also serves as a driver of current business behavior in the United States and, while it remains controversial, it was crafted as a result of chaos and a nebulous system that created obstacles for federal agencies trying to obtain information. International regulatory organizations like the Organisation of Economic Cooperation and Development (OECD), Transparency International (TI), Partnering Against Corruption Initiative (PACI), and a myriad of national organizations are increasingly making progress in setting a standard for the global market. The idea that integrity and business carry diverging values because company's only function in bottom line, net income-focused circumstances, is mistaken. Today's globalized world expects the existence of more integrity and the total revenue that your firm generates after costs and expenses can be directly traced back to your reputation as well as the reputation of those individuals and organizations that conduct business with you. My hope is that you and your company will use this practical guide as a tool to recognize the lessons learned. My review of significant fraud cases, legislative mandates, and governmental and non-governmental initiatives in the past 15 years should serve as examples and learning points. I review the negative cases and how it resulted in failed firms to find these lessons, but also examine those firms that continually survive fraudulent activities by senior management and/ or employees and have had their reputations slightly damaged and survived. This book will answer questions such as how do companies survive/fail in the face of fraud and corruption, why do they survive/fail despite fraud and corruption, and what can I do to protect/prevent a reputational crisis, among other crises, in my company? It is my belief that examining the experiences of prior companies' survival *and* failures will offer a better view of what to do in the face of a crisis that could lead to the dissolution of your company. The focus on the negative creates a one-sided argument and leads to immediate calls for regulation by the public and media. However, kneejerk responses almost never work when it comes to regulation. Entire industries have suffered the consequences of a few individuals and companies because regulations have stifled their ability to remain competitive in the global market. Therefore, highlighting how some companies have survived after crises and public relations disasters will help us understand those control systems that have worked. In each case, prevention was key and has saved shareholders, investors and industries immense costs as well as senior management and employees their jobs.

NEXT CHAPTERS

The following two chapters, Chapters 2 and 3, provide an analysis of business practices and regulatory environments in emerging and developed markets, respectively. More specifically, these chapters examine how markets are affected by globalization, cultural differences and corruption. The regulatory environments of the developed countries like Germany, the United Kingdom, United States and emerging markets like Brazil, China and Mexico will be discussed with examples of organizations, companies and individuals who attempt to scheme their way through compliance programs and risk their reputations, as well as their associates' reputations, to reap immediate financial rewards. However, these short-term rewards often carry lasting risks, higher financial costs and severely damage the reputations of individuals and companies involved as well as the entire global business community. Chapter 4 will focus on significant cases in the past 15 years that have affected legislation and the way we do business as a result of fraud and corruption. These cases will highlight how integrity and transparency were lacking in a few company structures and caused widespread damage to the business community that, in turn, led to over-regulation and a competitive disadvantage. Chapter 5 examines the drivers of current behavior such as the Foreign Corrupt Practices Act (FCPA), the Organisation for Economic Cooperation and Development (OECD), Transparency International (TI), Partnering Against Corruption Initiative (PACI) the United States Patriot Act, and Sarbanes–Oxley Act (SOX), the UK Bribery Act of 2010 and other governmental and non-governmental organizations and legislation that today regulate companies and individuals and demand adherence to business standards that promote integrity and transparency in business dealings. Adherence to these business standards is not only required to build confidence among companies and individuals doing business with each other, but they serve to fix a fragmented and uncertain system generated by globalization and lack of integrity. The final two chapters, Chapters 6 and 7, provide practical solutions and 'lessons learned' from fraud and corruption. While these solutions are continuously evolving, they will prepare your company and employees with the tools needed to consistently adapt and remain proactive in the face of corruption to ensure continuity and a positive reputation. The hope is that this practical guide results in better leadership within and across organizations, companies and individuals by introducing the idea that the coexistence of integrity and business in any organization is certainly possible.

CHAPTER TWO

EMERGING MARKETS

On 12 April 2012, the *New York Times* reported on its ongoing investigation about a potential Wal-Mart bribery scandal in Mexico and discovered 'a paper trail of hundreds of suspect payments totaling more than \$24 million' and a string of detailed e-mails where a 'former executive described how Wal-Mart de Mexico had orchestrated a campaign of bribery to win market dominance'.[1] These alleged bribes were made to procure zoning approvals, reduce environmental impact fees and gain the support of mayors, city council members, urban planners and other local bureaucrats who had the power to issue permits. The most deleterious finding was that executives at Wal-Mart de Mexico attempted to conceal records of these illicit payments from Wal-Mart headquarters in Bentonville, Arkansas as far back as September 2005. However, despite an investigative report by Wal-Mart's lead investigator, a former special agent at the US Federal Bureau of Investigations (FBI) who found there was 'reasonable suspicion to believe that Mexican and USA laws have been violated', Wal-Mart did not expand its investigation.[2] This has changed. In response to the *New York Times*' investigation and editorial, Wal-Mart initiated an internal investigation into potential Foreign Corrupt Practices Act (FCPA) violations and filed a statement with the US Securities Exchange Commission (US SEC), claiming 'we do not believe that these matters will have a material adverse effect on our business'.[3] In addition to the investigations by Wal-Mart and the US Department of Justice, the Mexican federal comptroller's office is also investigating these charges and has promised to hold accountable any and all public officials who are connected to this bribery scandal. In fact, Guillermo Tamborrel, a senator for President Felipe Calderón's National Action Party (PAN), claims that 'the scandal had tarnished Mexico's reputation' and 'we cannot let an international company come and corrupt our authorities'.[4] This case highlights a

---

1   David Barstow. 'Vast Mexico Bribery Case Hushed Up by Wal-Mart After Top-Level Struggle.' *New York Times*. 12 April 2012.
2   Ibid.
3   Ibid.
4   Miguel Gutierrez and Elinor Comlay. 'Mexico Starts Investigation in Wal-Mart Bribery Case.' Reuters. 25 April 2012.

few points I will discuss as we go further, particularly that conducting business in emerging markets entails more risks and demands on a company.

Regardless of the final results of the investigations by the US, Mexico and Wal-Mart authorities, there are already calls for more regulation. This is another point that this case highlights. As a result of the *New York Times'* investigation and report, there are already calls for stronger internal and external regulation. What we have to understand is that this is a typical, but reactive, response that follows every major case of fraud and corruption. In fact, in the *New York Times* article, David W. Tovar, Wal-Mart's spokesmen, already claimed that 'Wal-Mart is taking steps in Mexico to strengthen compliance with the Foreign Corrupt Practices Act' and that Wal-Mart 'will not tolerate noncompliance with FCPA anywhere or at any level of the company'.[5] This is fine. Companies must be aware of the rules and regulations that they must follow whether they are conducting business domestically or internationally. But, once again, the immediate reaction to fraud and corruption is more regulation rather than resolving the problem with a more long-term solution of prevention and internal policies and training that create a culture of accountability within a company. In any case, the damage control for Wal-Mart has already begun and it is the same call for more regulation that lacks a true seriousness of purpose. This bribery scandal has the potential to gain more publicity and not only materially harm Wal-Mart Mexico and the United States' reputations, but could also cause further mistrust in their political, social, cultural and economic relationships. Wal-Mart's bribery scandal also demonstrates how emerging markets are generally burdened in two ways: first, they do not have a strong regulatory and enforcement institutions and, second, because of the lack of a level playing field, certain companies are capable of taking advantage of the system, creating inefficiencies and additional cost instead of promoting competition and the best use of scarce resources. Fortunately, although late, the media served as a de facto regulator in this case and highlights the greater point that should be welcomed as a 'lesson learned' in the global business environment. The media, in addition to governmental and non-governmental regulators, function to expose corrupt practices today more than ever before in our history.

Wal-Mart's bribery scandal is capable of spoiling Mexico's reputation as an exemplary emerging market. Simply put, companies will shun markets where an unfair disadvantage exists and the only way to gain preferential treatment is through illegal means. Mexico is a key emerging market as well as one of three members of the North American Free Trade Agreement (NAFTA). Therefore, it is in the best interest of the United States, Mexico and Wal-Mart to resolve this issue quickly, hold those who attempted to conceal acts of bribery accountable and begin repairing their relationships. The benefit of the media's exposure of this corruption is that it has led Wal-Mart executives to push for reform. In fact, these

---

5   Ibid.

changes are not superficial, but quantifiable. Wal-Mart has promised regulators, its shareholders and the public that it will overhaul its regulatory system, put up a vote to possibly elect a new board, and hire more internal investigators. This demonstrates that transparency works and the importance of the media as a driver of current behavior. Instead of making forced, reactive calls for stronger regulations, we have to do a better job at understanding emerging markets, their risks in a global context, as well as cultural differences in business conduct. This will allow companies to set up strategies within their pre-existing compliance programs that will prevent and/or expose bribery and other forms of corruption. To do so, we have to identify how emerging markets function, how globalization functions and how companies are able to conduct business with integrity by arming themselves with beneficial knowledge through self-training on internal and external cultural issues and self-policing by building a culture of accountability.

WHAT ARE THE KEY CHARACTERISTICS OF EMERGING MARKETS?

How do we define emerging markets and why is it important? Making a precise list of emerging markets can be tricky because there are many ways we can define them, especially in a global context where there can be unexpected changes that can cause redefinition. In addition to the many ways that markets can be defined and redefined due to them being inexorably connected to political, social and cultural factors, the standards and process we use to define them add to the complexity. To offer simplicity, I utilize indices that provide a more encompassing definition of emerging markets and demonstrate how trade blocs and cooperation among markets helps us understand this transition into a globalized world. The five emerging market indices that are used to determine the classification of national economy as developed, emerging or less developed are the International Monetary Fund's (IMF) 'World Economic Outlook', the United Nations Development Programme's (UNDP) 'Human Development Report', and the *Financial Times* and Stock Exchange (FTSE), Morgan Stanley Capital Investment (MSCI) and Banco Bilbao Vizcaya Argentaria (BBVA) financial market indices.[6] The first two, IMF's 'World Economic Outlook' and UNDP's 'Human Development Report', provide comparative analyses of economic development and policies in their member countries, the international financial market and the global economic system. Furthermore, and necessary to this discussion regarding the increase of business being conducted in multicultural and trans-jurisdictional settings, the UNDP's 'Human Development Report' provides an analysis of how economic

---

6   World Economic and Financial Surveys. *World Economic Outlook: Growth Resuming, Dangers Remain.* International Monetary Fund (IMF). Washington, DC. April 2012. Human Development Report. *Sustainability and Equity: A Better Future for All.* United Nations Development Programme (UNDP). New York, New York. HDR 2011.

development impacts standards of living. The next three market indices are developed by FTSE, MSCI and BBA whose experts classify national economies by using different parameters, but consistently arrive at similar conclusions regarding market status. The above five emerging market indices provide a stronger means of classifying countries as developed, developing and less developed. Together, they provide a platform for sound comparative analyses of the important sectors (i.e., the political, social, cultural factors and financial sectors) required to properly measure the global marketplace.

Emerging markets are national economies that are in positive transition, are undergoing rapid growth and are 'emerging' as key players in the global business community. The leading emerging markets today are Brazil, China, Egypt, India, Indonesia, Mexico, Russia, South Africa, South Korea and Turkey. These markets are not only experiencing economic growth, but also changes in their political, social and cultural activities. This chapter examines emerging markets in the context of globalization and the heightened risk of fraud and corruption in these markets. With the premise that fraud and corruption affects us all, I focus on how companies must be aware of two important trends. First, emerging markets have established themselves as important actors in the global market economy. Second, companies conducting business in emerging markets sometimes have a negative incentive to do so. The importance of new and emerging markets is not only evidenced in the growth of multinational corporations and more companies conducting business in these markets, but also evidenced in the increase of countries that have emerging markets qualifying for and/or gaining memberships to trade blocs in the past 20 years (see Table 2.1). This is economic globalization where more integration, cooperation and comparable advantages are achieved. Gaining membership to trade blocs is important in a globalized world because it not only provides more legitimacy as a stable market and attracts a larger business presence, but also reduces some barriers to the exchange of goods and services that benefits companies. What this increase in membership to trade blocs also tells us is that emerging markets are becoming commoditized and more central to multinational corporations' business plans. Trade blocs have stipulations that mandate compliance to economic regulations as part of its membership requirements. Unfortunately, these do not always govern issues of fraud and corruption. Thus, conducting business in emerging markets presents the highest risk for companies because compliance standards are often perceived as laxer than in more developed markets or simply ignored by companies attempting to gain an unfair advantage.

Aside from human development and market indices to identify emerging markets, experts have also clustered them into loosely defined groups that vary from large to very small markets. For example, banking and financial institutions have particularly assigned acronyms and labels to designate emerging market blocs such as BRIC (i.e., Brazil, Russia, India and China), CIVETS (i.e., Colombia, Indonesia,

Table 2.1   List of key trade blocs and their members

Year	Trade Bloc	Members and Observers
1991	Common Southern Market (Mercosur)	Members: Argentina, Brazil, Paraguay, Uruguay and Venezuela. Associate Members: Bolivia, Chile, Colombia, Ecuador and Peru. Observers: Mexico, New Zealand
1991	Central American Integration System (SICA)	Members: Belize, Dominican Republic (associated state), Guatemala, El Salvador, Honduras, Nicaragua, Costa Rica, Panama. Observers: Mexico, Chile, Brazil, China, Spain, Germany and Japan
1992	ASEAN Free Trade Area (AFTA)	Members: Brunei, Indonesia, Malaysia, Philippines, Singapore, Thailand, Myanmar, Cambodia, Laos and Vietnam. Observers: Australia, China, India, Japan, New Zealand, Papua New Guinea, South Korea and Timor-Leste
1993	European Union; formerly the European Economic Community under the Treaty of Paris (1952) and the Treaty of Rome (1958)	Members: Austria, Belgium, Bulgaria, Cyprus, Czech Republic, Denmark, Estonia, Finland, France, Germany, Greece, Hungary, Ireland, Italy, Latvia, Lithuania, Luxembourg, Malta, Netherlands, Poland, Portugal, Romania, Slovakia, Slovenia, Spain, Sweden and United Kingdom
1994	North American Free Trade Agreement (NAFTA)	Members: Canada, Mexico, United States
1994	Common Market for Eastern and Southern Africa (COMESA)	Members: Burundi, Comoros, Democratic Republic of the Congo, Djibouti, Egypt, Eritrea, Ethiopia, Kenya, Libya, Madagascar, Malawi, Mauritius, Rwanda, Seychelles, South Sudan, Sudan, Swaziland, Uganda, Zambia, Zimbabwe
1998	Greater Arab Free Trade Agreement (GAFTA); formerly, the Council of Arab Economic Unity (CAEU) founded in 1957	Members: Algeria, Bahrain, Egypt, Iraq, Jordan, Kuwait, Lebanon, Libya, Morocco, Oman, Palestinian territories, Qatar, Saudi Arabia, Sudan, Syria, Tunisia, United Arab Emirates, Yemen
2004	South Asian Free Trade Agreement (SAFTA)	Members: Bangladesh, Bhutan, India, Maldives, Nepal, Pakistan, Afghanistan and Sri Lanka
2006	Trans-Pacific Partnership (TPP)	Members: Brunei, Chile, New Zealand and Singapore. Negotiating to Join the Group: Australia, Malaysia, Peru, Japan, United States and Vietnam
2007	Central European Free Trade Agreement (CEFTA)	Members: Albania, Bosnia and Herzegovina, Croatia, Macedonia, Moldova, Montenegro, Serbia and UNMIK on behalf of Kosovo. Former Members (now EU): Bulgaria, Czech Republic, Hungary, Poland, Romania, Slovakia and Slovenia

Vietnam, Egypt, Turkey and South Africa), or the Next Eleven (Bangladesh, Egypt, Indonesia, Iran, Mexico, Nigeria, Pakistan, Philippines, South Korea, Turkey and Vietnam). These acronyms and labels, while they may not signify anything other than a more simplified way that denotes and separates these emerging markets from other markets, represent financial targets and opportunities. In any case, emerging markets all together represent 83 per cent of the world's economies and are fast-growing. Accordingly, just as developed market economies like the United States, United Kingdom, Germany and Japan are very different from each other, so are emerging markets. Some emerging markets, like Brazil and China, have more economic diversity *within* them than most developed economies in total; they not only represent the largest emerging markets, but they bring many varied markets with them. In fact, the Chinese economy itself is already considered a global economic power with positive market potential, despite having vast areas of underdevelopment. This is not only intriguing from a business perspective where the possibilities of new goods and services serves as incentives to enter these markets, but also adds to the complexity of trying to define them in a more a specific way.

Many emerging market projections are focused on economic rise and market potential rather than on the overall development of a market, all together dismissing political and social changes that occur more erratically in some countries. In addition, the risk of fraud and corruption often goes unheeded. Thus, prior to engaging in business in an emerging market, companies should go beyond reviewing their potential associate's financial, legal and industrial status and analyze the market from a holistic and comparative perspective. A holistic and comparative analysis will answer critical questions about the market such as: did prior companies encounter obstacles when entering into the market? What were these obstacles? Is there a history of resistance against foreign investments? Is there resistance to change? Will there be any issues adjusting to new global, regulatory standards in this market? Unfortunately, these analyses are not guaranteed to offer a sure-fire solution to every potential challenge because there is limited knowledge about emerging markets.

Many of these emerging markets do not have a history of stability as part of an open market system and certainly not in a globalized one. After all, they are still 'emerging.' Yet, they are geographically and demographical intriguing and their diversity in products and services provide incentives for future investors. For instance, Brazil and China will be the first emerging markets that will have larger economies than most of their developed counterparts in the next 10 years according to market projections. These two emerging markets will not only have more influence in the global market economy but also largely affect political and social platforms in developed markets. Certainly, we cannot expect emerging markets to change their ways of conducting business and adhere to global standards without having any input. Companies in emerging markets today can initiate changes, set precedents and ensure business is conducted with integrity in the future.

EMERGING MARKETS AND CORRUPTION

Based on the list of key trade blocs and their members (Table 2.1), and the data collected by the IMF's 'World Economic Outlook,' UNDP's 'Human Development Report,' and the FTSE, MSCI, and BBVA's financial market indices, of the 120 countries in these key trade blocs, 17 per cent are developed, 43 per cent are emerging markets, 40 per cent consists of frontier or less-developed markets (see Figure 2.1).

This is an indication of the growing importance of new and emerging markets in the global business community. In the past 20 years, companies in developed markets have increasingly offshored their business to new and emerging markets. Offshoring has improved the economy of both developed and emerging markets, evidenced by growth in each markets' overall gross domestic product figures. However, although these cooperating markets have experienced growth in the global economy, the risk of fraud and corruption has also increased. The increase in corruption in emerging markets was a leading concern of the *United Nations Convention Against Corruption* report in 2003 whereby former Secretary General of the United Nations, Kofi Annan, called attention to corruption in the developing world, claiming:

> *Corruption is an insidious plague that has a wide range of corrosive effects on societies. It undermines democracy and the rule of law, leads to violations of human rights, distorts markets, erodes the quality of life and allows organized crime, terrorism and other threats to human security to flourish.*
>
> *This evil phenomenon is found in all countries—big and small, rich and poor—but it is in the developing world that its effects are most destructive. Corruption hurts the poor disproportionately by diverting funds intended for development, undermining a Government's ability to provide basic services, feeding inequality and injustice and discouraging foreign aid and investment. Corruption is a key element in economic underperformance and a major obstacle to poverty alleviation and development.[7]*

---

7   Foreword of the *United Nations Convention Against Corruption*. Kofi Annan. United Nations Office on Drugs and Crime. New York, New York. 31 October 2003. Also, 'New Instrument Described as New Framework for Action against "Insidious Plague"' (press release). United Nations, New York. 31 October 2003.

Market Percentage in Key Trade Blocs

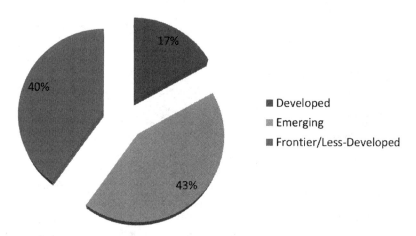

Figure 2.1   Market percentage in key trade blocs

The political and economic frameworks in developing markets offered lesser incentives for companies to reduce corruption for two related reasons: first, there was often an absence of economic incentives to reduce corruption. When conducting business in another country that lacks the necessary regulatory structure to prevent corruption, companies sensed that circumventing the rules and regulations was part of the normal course of business. That is, a culture of corruption was normalized and built upon companies witnessing each other gain unfair advantage in these markets by finding ways to sidestep existing regulations. The second reason was that, for many years, there had been weak enforcement once corruption was discovered. Companies weighed their costs and preferred to take the risks of being discovered, paying insignificant fines and penalties, and simply get a slap on the wrist when compared to the benefit of winning a bid and getting contracts. Fortunately, this has changed and it no longer benefits companies to take these risks. The solutions are varied, but we can particularly point at three changes that have occurred which are directly caused by globalization: the rise of social media as an external regulator, stiffer penalties that outweigh the risks of attempting to commit fraud—particularly, bribing officials—via legislation, and the increase in the amount of governmental and non-governmental organizations that monitor and increase awareness of corruption such as Transparency International (TI), Partnering Against Corruption Initiatives (PACI), and the United Nations Convention Against Corruption.[8]

---

8   These organizations, the media, and domestic and international legislation will be the subject of Chapter 5: Drivers of Current Behavior where I demonstrate how these changes have combined to thwart corrupt behavior and have caused companies to begin policing

There are many incentives to conducting business in new and emerging markets, particularly the obvious benefits of lower operating costs to companies and taking advantage of the benefits of global resources. This includes proven gains in productivity, efficiency, quality and revenues when companies successfully leverage their offshore talent. Alternatively, there are also incentives for countries with emerging markets to attract business by any means necessary. This is where the issue of corruption should be addressed. The problem is that these incentives are sometimes either unethical, but legal, or outright illegal. In more instances, the legality of these incentives is unclear because their laws are either concurrently developing alongside its market or because of differences in cultural perspectives regarding business conduct. The reduced barriers to the exchange of goods and services within trade blocs often provide developed, emerging and under-developed markets a comparative advantage, one that is surely not overlooked by companies that are deciding where to expand their business. However, entering a new market means that your company must be prepared and properly informed about its investments and avoid the potential problem of corruption. Economic risks aside, companies have to be aware of the political, social and cultural risks.

Emerging markets usually have different standards of conducting business and, while forms of bribery may be an accepted part of business in them, the laws of your country of origin may still govern your company. For instance, the US FCPA and the newly passed UK Bribery Act of 2010 emphasize the requirement that companies who do business, in any capacity, in the United States and United Kingdom must adhere to its anti-corruption and anti-bribery stipulations. The UK Bribery Act of 2010 goes even further, prohibiting bribes paid between privately held entities instead of limiting it just to the interaction with government officials. Therefore, even if a business practice is merely considered unethical or part of normal business conduct in another market, United States and United Kingdom companies are still governed by FCPA and Bribery Act laws. These laws help transcend the potential of cultural differences in business conduct by providing a fair and balanced field and increasing integrity, although some entrepreneurs believe it places them at a competitive disadvantage. Summing up, cultural differences are growing risks that cannot be ignored because they have the potential to negatively affect a company's reputation, lead to fines and penalties, expensive litigation and, in the most severe case, a company's collapse.

GLOBALIZATION, EMERGING MARKETS AND CULTURE

The effects of globalization and how it has given rise to new and emerging markets cannot be understated. One of the features of globalization that professional

themselves by strengthening their internal control systems and placing more focus on their compliance programmes.

practitioners should be more cognizant of is how cultural differences may affect the way we conduct business. Companies conducting business in a different market than their own are expected to train and make their professionals aware of these differences in culture. In fact, your company and professionals will benefit from recognizing how ethical and integrity issues are uniquely associated with a better understanding of each other's cultural differences and how to make it work in a globalized world. Business integrity issues involve knowing how differences in culture affect everyday business practices, not only in new and emerging markets, but also in developed markets. Globalization entails greater cooperation, especially in increasingly multicultural and trans-jurisdictional business settings. Thus, by attaining greater knowledge of how culture affects business practices, companies can prevent setbacks to their reputations and market values. One of the main causes of unethical and/or illegal business practices is that we are unaware and untrained at dealing with cultural differences. Gaining awareness of these cultural differences requires us to change business practices and, as we know, change is a difficult thing for most companies. Yet, globalization requires change. In order to benefit from the vast array of new conveniences and capabilities that a globalized business community offers, companies have to streamline their compliance programs. Today's compliance programs require solutions for the challenges that emerging markets, and their inbuilt multicultural settings, produce.

The process of globalization demands that companies conducting business in emerging markets, where there is typically an intersection among different standards, regulations and business cultures, to be aware of the cultural risks involved. This does not imply that cultures in emerging markets do not value standards and integrity in business conduct as much as their more developed counterparts, nor does it imply the need for a 'universal' cultural ethic to be imposed on the various cultures and countries within emerging markets. On the contrary, successful companies in both markets have learned to adapt to the different circumstances that globalization has provided and do not lack comprehension of the standards created. In fact, successful companies, those that have spotless reputations and increased market values, also have a strong comprehension of cultural differences and are more disinclined to conduct business with those individuals and companies that have a history of crossing ethical boundaries. These companies do not always make headlines, but they exist. According to the Ethisphere Institute, there has been an increase in the number of companies 'that show leadership in promoting ethical business standards'.[9] In fact, not only are more companies 'exceeding legal minimums for compliance', but they are also 'forcing their competitors to follow

---

9   'Ethisphere Recognizes Exceptional Ethical Leadership at The Global Ethics Summit and World's Most Ethical (WME) Companies Honoree Dinner in New York' (press release) Ethisphere Institute. New York, New York. 15 March 2012. For Ethisphere Institute's list of the World's Most Ethical Companies, go to http://www.ethisphere.com/wme/.

suit'.[10] The surge in companies operating more ethically, and with greater integrity, demonstrates that the global market community is improving on its awareness of cultural risks when conducting business in emerging markets.

Globalization is a transitory process that affects the political, economic and social arenas in both emerging and developed markets. For this reason, the stakes are higher. Conducting business in new and emerging markets not only contains greater risks for companies already engaged in these markets, but also for companies who wish to do so in the future. If patterns of fraud and corruption exist, it sets a precedent for subsequent companies and their practitioners. As each case of fraud and corruption shows, accountability is often passed on to others who conducted business in the same manner, but none escaped liability. Emerging markets are making the world unfamiliar and the importance of cultural understanding, those behaviors and beliefs that are characteristic of a particular group, is more valuable to companies today. There are greater risks today and it can be said, with justification, that overcoming cultural differences minimizes these risks. The topic of business ethics and integrity issues is relatable in all markets. Every professional today deals with intersecting cultures and/or diverse behaviors and beliefs of people at all levels of the marketplace. This is good for the global market community. These changes and differences are far from damaging and the benefits outweigh the risks, especially because all companies and markets are in constant transition and seeking new products and services that help their bottom line. However, when corruption occurs, ascertaining what went wrong, fixing the damage and/or preventing recurring issues of corruption demands that we accept these differences and produce a culture of accountability within our companies rather than attempting to create a universal standard through more regulation. We currently have a stronger system than media headlines reveal and integrity is built on companies' willingness to change rather than by force.

The problem with a cultural analysis of globalization and business acumen is that it runs the risk of becoming moralistic and angles itself into a comparative view of values. This is not the case in this analysis. In the general sense, culture is difficult to define because it is never permanent, but constantly evolving and it makes it all but impossible to evaluate culture as a quantifiable variable. Yet, with a more specific viewpoint, culture is what produces an incentive to go into new and emerging markets, develop them, and gain from the collaborative experience with integrity. The benefits of economic globalization, its ability to have different markets collaborate and cooperative to produce better goods and services, complements the unprecedented number of cultural knowledge brought about by media technologies. It is not only an issue of multiculturalism in business, but also equality of access to information that can be important to fighting corruption. Globalization of the market economy does not require a 'culture' to change. In

---

10   Ibid.

fact, cultural differences make it more compelling for investors because different markets provide new opportunities. An ethical foundation is required to achieve economic cooperation and it begins with companies taken on the responsibility to promote cultural literacy and a culture of accountability within their workforce, regardless of their market.

CONCLUSION

Emerging markets share significant commonalities in spite of their diversity. They each have initiated a move towards greater economic development by opening themselves up to the global market and captivating foreign investors, including becoming more transparent, achieving efficiency and having dependable performance levels. These changes include reforming their previous economic models to build investor confidence. Certainly, many emerging markets, specifically the smaller ones, do not have the resources to regulate themselves or simply do not have any incentives to call for more reform. Unfortunately, part of this disincentive comes from investors who want minimal regulations in order to create and maintain an advantage over this new market capital. The global economy is irrefutably more integrated today than at any time in history and adverse events in any corner of the world is more likely to have a sizeable global impact. Thus, our unfamiliarity with today's integrated environment necessitates a stronger and more holistic understanding beyond the global economy that includes political, social and culture factors in order to preserve integrity and secure a stronger platform for development.

One of the key risks in doing business in emerging markets is that it offers limited protection against corruption. There are different expectations across the global market. As emerging markets grow and alter pre-established global standards of business set by their more developed counterparts, companies need to adjustment to these changes and challenge instances of corruption. All multinational companies bear the added pressure to reduce their risks in unregulated emerging markets. The highest priority, and the most difficult to accomplish on a broader scale, is to identify the causes of corruption in both markets and take measures to eliminate the incentives. More specifically, this can be accomplished by refusing to conduct business with entities and/or individuals that have questionable pasts, request illicit payments, and/or conduct business in a manner that *your* company's rules and regulations deem unethical. This is the essence of self-policing and building a culture of accountability. For example, Wal-Mart could have prevented an external investigation by the *New York Times* that brought about allegations that its leadership in Arkansas attempted to conceal corruption, by executives charged at their Wal-Mart de Mexico subsidiary, if they followed their internal control system's measures. Wal-Mart's compliance program had these preventative measures in place. Yet, those entrusted in leadership positions and were capable of facing these allegations, finding an internal resolution, and avoiding greater financial, legal and reputational costs, simply chose to ignore them. The challenge for Wal-Mart is now threefold. As with any case of fraud and corruption, the first challenge is to determine how this occurred and what needs to be fixed in order to prevent these damaging and illegal events from happening again. The second challenge is now coping with the results of both the US Department of Justice and Mexico's federal comptroller's investigations. The third challenge is repairing the damage to Wal-Mart's overall reputation, not only in Mexico and United States, but also globally. These will all be very costly, much more than the estimated $25 million dollars in bribes that were allegedly doled out to Mexican officials.

The effects of globalization can create animosities, especially when cultural differences are involved. There is no perfect market system that operates without flaws. Institutions responsible for regulation and enforcement of the law are weak, under resourced and inefficient, making it difficult for an ethical company to compete with corrupt (and often local) competitors. However, this is changing at a rapid pace. Companies now find themselves policed by their home markets and increasingly under scrutiny by regulatory and enforcement authorities in the emerging markets in which they operate. The stakes are getting higher, and this is driving the need to ensure ethical behavior across the spectrum of markets in which companies operate.

Globalization does not require a perfectly standard market in order to function, but one that requires all markets to get involved and understand the global impact of economic, political and social differences. Developed markets are assumed to be less risky because they have stronger compliance systems based on regulatory mandates, have more stable and high-income economies and have broader market liquidity to support global investments. However, businesses in these markets have not always been the best trailblazers. Fortunately, most companies in both markets are not willing to risk the rewards of investing in markets that do not have appropriate standards or any anti-corruption regulations in place prior to engaging in business because the negative effects, particularly as financial and reputation costs are increasingly significant. Thus, it is crucial that companies in developed and emerging markets initiate an internal commitment towards promoting ethical conduct and safeguarding investments.

CHAPTER THREE

DEVELOPED MARKETS

The most common scenario one imagines in dealing with problems arising from ethics and compliance lapses in companies is that of companies entering developing markets and not imposing their culture. While being subjected to weak regulatory laws and lack of enforcement of the same and coupled with the pressures of trying not to do 'business as usual', companies may succumb to the pressures to cut corners. However, it is equally true that there have been a large number of major occurrences of fraud and ethics lapses of companies in their own home developed markets that went undetected for years and were only uncovered by severe market drops. Examples such as Enron, Madoff, Stanford Bank, Drier and MF Global remind us that the threat to company's reputation and integrity isn't just found in difficult to navigate emerging markets abroad.

In Chapter 2, I discussed the risks involved when conducting business in emerging markets and showed how companies can build accountability, transparency and place more efforts in their due diligence processes to eschew corrupt business practices. My objective is to provide a practical guideline for companies and practitioners conducting business in all markets and examine the risks and obligations necessary to run an effective company in a globalized world, even in the face of a crisis where continuity is increasingly dependent on your reputation. An examination of the complexities of emerging markets is incomplete without examining developed markets as well. This chapter advises companies and professional practitioners in developed markets to also concentrate their efforts on the fundamental elements of anti-corruption strategies in building accountability, transparency and firmer reputational due diligence processes. Thus, how are developed markets defined today?

All definitions of emerging and developed markets will not conform to each of these measures and have differing characteristics. For instance, despite China clearly being an emerging market if we consider economic growth and potential as the criteria, it is home to some of the world's largest companies and is fast gaining influence in the global business market. However, from a compliance, regulatory and business integrity standpoint, China is clearly a part of the developing world with all its requisite challenges. One major obstacle to its development of a culture of oversight and probity is the fact that most of China's largest and most influential companies are SOEs (state-owned enterprises).[1] Adhering to global regulatory standards requires a more open market and China's closed market is clearly a challenge that cannot be ignored for those who are working to resolve the problem of global corruption. At every level, less transparency leads to the potential for fraud and corruption to happen. In addition, this lack of regulatory authorities and transparency manifests itself in other areas such as employment, quality control, and/or environmental standards. As a result of the negative publicity about China's low-waged workers, faulty products and environmental standards, companies are more apprehensive about conducting business in China. However, interest in China remains unchanged. It is a juggernaut and, as the value of accountability, anti-graft efforts, and transparency in a globalized world become more evident, China will realize that the benefits these fundamental elements of business integrity bring with them are substantial. China represents the front line between the key characteristics of emerging and developed markets. It is an interesting phenomenon, onee that will continue to evolve in the next decade. The following section provides an outline of the characteristics used to define developed markets, which new and emerging markets can use to measure themselves against.

WHAT ARE THE KEY CHARACTERISTICS OF DEVELOPED MARKETS?

As discussed, developed markets are not immune from the instabilities that corruption produces. While more developed markets typically offer companies and investors security and stability, concerted and sophisticated efforts to subvert their regulations and enforcement agencies are often successful. However, all together defined, developed markets have an array of commonalities that make them unlike emerging markets. More specifically, fraud and corruption are common occurrences in all markets. While acts of corruption may be vastly different (i.e., bribery, insider trading, Ponzi Schemes, etc.), they equally impact the global marketplace. This is why developed markets are not immune to the instabilities caused by corruption. In a globalized world, there are no isolated incidents. Although developed markets may have more stringent rules and regulations and better oversight, this does not necessarily provide a guarantee that corruption is less likely to occur in them. More importantly, their effects are exponentially greater because they are home to the world's largest companies. Thus, companies must allocate proper resources to these markets as well and not simply rely on government agencies or third parties to handle this for them. The following are five characteristics that help identify developed markets:

---

1   China Petroleum & Chemical Corporation Limited (Sinopec Group), China National Petroleum Corporation (CNPC), and State Grid Corporation of China (SGCC) are in the Top 10 of the world's largest companies and are each state-owned enterprises.

1. Developed markets have comparatively stable economic growth and are considered high-income economies, particularly yielding high per capita income and gross domestic product rates.
2. Developed markets have obtained levels of industrialization, infrastructural development and a standard of living that reflects its economic stability.
3. Developed markets are home to the world's largest companies and these companies have the largest foreign assets.
4. Developed markets have comparatively tougher regulatory authorities and have allocated a sizeable workforce towards them.
5. Developed markets, because of stricter regulations, have built strong mechanisms to achieve accountability and transparency, including having effective and efficient reporting processes.

According to economic analysts with established criteria for determining developed markets, there is consensus among them that there are 26 countries with developed markets, with 5 more markets making the list.[2] These are markets carrying the least risks because they have substantial size, wealth and market depth and breadth (see Table 3.1).

These developed economies possess the five characteristics of developed economies that I have outlined above; stability, levels of industrial and infrastructural development that yield high standards of living, the world's largest companies, strong regulatory authorities and stronger mechanisms to achieve accountability and transparency than emerging markets. Yet, there is a critical point that needs to be emphasized: developed markets are also experiencing a transition because global regulatory standards have changed the way they conduct business as well. That is, developed markets are experiencing changes along with new and emerging markets, often with resistance towards these changes because they are perceived as overly onerous and costly.

Developed and emerging markets also resist change because standardization conflicts with their local customs and traditional ways of conducting business. These struggles caused by change facilitate discourse among regulators, the media and the public about the challenges of conducting business in a globalized world, including helping to find solutions to these challenges. Unfortunately, companies and markets are most vulnerable to corruption during transitory periods. Thus, some individuals have treated this transitory period (i.e., globalization and changes due to new and emerging markets) as an opportunity to commit fraud and corruption by finding ways to circumvent the system without attracting notice, making developed markets just as vulnerable to fraud and corruption as emerging markets. It is as if a rock

---

2   Sources: Financial Times and Stock Exchange International Ltd (FTSE Group), Morgan Stanley Capital International (MSCI), Standard and Poor's (S&P), Dow Jones & Company, and Russell Investments.

Table 3.1   List of developed markets

List of developed markets		
Consensus:	Australia	Japan
	Austria	Luxembourg
	Belgium	Netherlands
	Canada	New Zealand
	Denmark	Norway
	Finland	Portugal
	France	Singapore
	Germany	South Korea
	Greece	Spain
	Hong Kong	Sweden
	Ireland	Switzerland
	Israel	United Kingdom
	Italy	United States
Also classified:	Cyprus	Slovenia
	Iceland	Taiwan
	Malta	

has been unturned: simultaneously revealing a world of unprecedented opportunities in the marketplace with unforeseen, and occasionally sordid and corrupt behavior, business conduct. There is a remedy. It begins by understanding our regulatory environment with a global perspective. Corruption is not new, but has evolved and become more complex. By making sense of these newly minted characteristics of corruption and adapting our traditional business strategies to counter them, we can quickly expose and self-regulate corrupt conduct.

DEVELOPED MARKETS AND EMERGING MARKETS IN TRANSITION

The influx of new and emerging markets, seemingly irrelevant in the past, is now spearheading the move towards a globalized and interconnected business system. Many of the issues that face both markets parallel each other or are inexorable processes. The general belief is that new and emerging markets have a more difficult time adjusting to the regulatory structures of developed markets, but the impacts are the same. Developed markets are also having a difficult time transitioning into a globalized business world. That is, there is a fundamental misunderstanding between developed and emerging markets in relation to what should be exemplary business conduct. Both markets are forced to mix their familiar traditions in business conduct with elements that the global economy commands; market integration, cooperation and integrity are essential to conducting business in a globalized world. There is a misunderstanding about the intentions behind regulation because we rely on comparative terms like developed, emerging (developing) and frontier/less-developed markets. These are value-laden views of the relationship among professionals, companies and the marketplace in both markets. The conflict during transitional periods arises from what is the right and wrong way to conduct business. This produces limiting solutions because it does not lead to cooperation. Instead, it is a power struggle between traditions and which market wins out. We have to avoid moralizing about which business processes and regulations are better and achieve a business model that is built on cooperation against corruption. It is in the interest of all parties to abide by existing regulations designed to prevent corruption.

Companies in developed and emerging markets should encourage and demand non-corrupt and ethical business practices because they each provide materially significant advantages to the global marketplace. If your business partners do not have a good reputation, simply do not conduct business with them. This is the premise of self-regulation. What makes the global market unfamiliar, and fittingly causes apprehension, is not necessarily the differences between markets but that globalization is unprecedented in history. By not doing business with a questionable business partner, the unpredictability is minimized; shareholders and potential investors who have done their due diligence notice these decisions. This transition into a globalized business community has been unpredictable and, therefore, requires professionals at the immediate level to make decisions that are built on integrity. Even if it means a short-term loss of revenue, the long-term benefits of conducting business with integrity are evidenced in the success of many top-flight companies in developed and emerging markets who have refused to put their reputations and companies on the line and are spearheading anti-graft and anti-corruption efforts. In fact, it can be argued that top-flight companies in both markets support regulatory structures that enhance long-term stability and revenue. There will always be risks in business, but this is what makes the upside of rewards greater than the downside of risks; new and emerging markets contain opportunities for new products, services and revenue when your company properly complies with all levels of compliance and regulates itself. Self-regulation is key to minimizing risks that could further destabilize the market. However, the market demands cooperation against graft and corruption because less-regulated areas will be flushed with those who want to avoid more regulated markets.

DEVELOPED MARKETS AND CORRUPTION

Corruption tends to be more common and complex than most other negative events that companies will face because they have a greater, negative impact on reputation. Reputation cannot be bifurcated from companies' business strategies. Therefore, companies in developed markets have to be a driving force of global ethical standards because they currently have the most influence in generating a reputation that is thoroughly based on integrity. Recent developments in global regulatory standards increase the risk of your company and/or professionals of being accused of corruption.[3] In short, there are a few aspects of business practices that carry as many risks, or in which the stakes are so high, as conducting business without a level of transparency and a uniform set of regulatory standards. This does not necessarily mean that global regulatory standards are to be set by developed markets without any input from emerging markets. In fact, emerging markets are contributing to these standards. Companies in developed markets have their problems following regulatory and ethical standards as well; and, these have produced the darkest, most problematic episodes in the history of the global financial system.[4] The regulatory failures exposed after the 2008 financial crisis led to an avalanche of global effects that still resonate as the case against whether integrity exists in business.

The 2008 bailouts as a result of the United States financial crisis and the perceived 'unsustainability' of the Eurozone, which prompted a *reversal* of its bailout policy with the establishment of the European Stability Mechanism (ESM) to assist Eurozone countries in financial despair, contribute to the notion that there is a need for reform. Moreover, combined with the increase exposure of fraud and corruption by companies in developed markets in the past decade, it is not a surprise that many believe we are falling over the edge with so many elements out of balance. Reforms are certainly needed and are inevitable; and, there are many examples of how minor adjustments to business strategies as a result of fraud have led to more confidence and integrity in our system. Nonetheless, the recent bailouts in two of the largest economies in the world as well as our experience with corruption in recent year, have led to ill-advised calls for tougher regulation in all markets. This comes from the belief that everyone will benefit from more regulation. This is partly correct, but is equally a blind understanding of how the market really works. It is correct that when compliance is observed, in any capacity or level

---

3   This is further examined in Chapter 5: Drivers of Current Behavior.
4   This is further examined in Chapter 4: Case Studies of Major Fraud and Corruption Around the World.

of the marketplace, everyone benefits. However, too much regulation will stifle competition, especially if everyone is not on board.

The US Dodd-Frank Act and UK Bribery Act of 2010 are the toughest legislation against corruption and are clearly helpful; they promote accountability, transparency and stability in the financial system. However, we must not interrupt and limit honest business risks, which have been beneficial for the economy. A proper balance is needed if we are to keep all markets fairly competitive. We have confused risk-taking, a normal part of doing business, with corruption when it does not benefit risk-takers and/or when their investments do not pay off as they anticipated. This is equally damaging because it places reputations at stake, despite a lack of wrongdoing. Risk-taking failure in the market is not corruption. We are also confusing unpredictable changes caused by globalization with corruption.

The alleged 'unsustainability' of the Eurozone as currently structured, and the need to bail out some of its members, is due to macroeconomic root causes and not the product of corruption. Prior to economic integration, it was known that there is a potential some members of the Eurozone may need financial help, specifically southern European countries like Greece, Italy, Portugal and Spain, which were less developed than the others. Needless to say, the Eurozone is still evolving as predicted back in the late 1990s, but it is far from unsustainable. In both cases, the US and Eurozone, these have market forces that cannot be patched up with mere reform in the shape of more regulation. It has to come within the business community's ability to self-regulate. In order to achieve a culture of accountability, transparency and ethical conduct, companies (and countries) and their processes have to be strengthened internally rather than cuffed by more regulatory authority. Corruption involves patterns of misconduct and unethical behavior. It is a controllable circumstance and very few corrupt companies and professionals have bypassed existing regulations. Adding more regulations will resolve this existing pattern, but not the misconduct nor unethical behavior born out of lack of transparency and accountability within a company or a few individuals who act as if their material interests are greater than the law. Again, not all failed business conduct and risks are due to corruption.

Let us briefly examine the case of Facebook, Inc.'s highly publicized initial public offering (IPO) on 17 May 2012. Only days after its IPO, Facebook, Inc. was being investigated by the US SEC, the Financial Industry Regulatory Authority (FIRA), and the US Senate Banking Committee, among other authorities, to determine how the IPO was handled and whether or not Facebook, Inc. told its underwriters to 'materially lower its forecast for the company' and to disclose these 'lowered forecasts to 'preferred' investors only, instead of all investors'.[5] Companies can be

---

5   Jonathan Stempel and Dan Levine. 'Facebook, Banks Sued Over Pre-IPO Analyst Calls.' *Reuters*. UK Edition. 24 March 2012.

held criminally liable for lying or omitting pertinent information during the US SEC registration process and can be prosecuted for deceiving investors. These reports have renewed demand for regulation, anti-graft efforts and affected the financial industry's reputation. The case in point: in a lawsuit filed by three Facebook, Inc. shareholders, Bank of America Corporation, Barclays PLC, Goldman Sachs, JP Morgan Chase and Morgan Stanley are named as defendants along with Facebook, Inc.'s CEO Mark Zuckerberg.[6] Although this case is still evolving, there are a couple of takeaways that highlight the issues that we have been discussing (or will discuss in the following chapters) regarding: reputation, transparency and regulation. First, cases of fraud and corruption, including the 2008 financial crisis, have left a lasting stain on the reputation on the entire business community. Surely, this highly publicized IPO was going to be highly scrutinized. Regardless of the outcome, this has affected Facebook, Inc. and its underwriters' reputations to some degree. There are now panicked efforts to withdraw investments in Facebook, Inc. and its shares are already facing volatility, having dropped 25 per cent of its value in the first 10 days. This will stabilize, but the initial charges of corrupt business practices and lack of transparency will remain. What has not gained enough attention is how quickly these charges are being investigated and how existing control mechanisms are working. This is significant because it shows how the current regulatory environment, particularly as a result of media technologies, immediately manages these charges of unethical business conduct.

The issue of transparency is once again a key element of the fine line between ethical and unethical business conduct. If Facebook, Inc. and its underwriters were selectively disclosing material facts that included negative information to some investors then the argument that there was a lack of transparency is valid. But it also lends legitimacy to the current regulatory environment because it was immediately managed. Nevertheless, if the charges are legitimate in this case, and the odds were stacked against investors without preferred connections on Wall Street, then further damage to the business community's reputation can be expected. The omission of important facts, selectively disclosing negative findings, and false statements on the IPO statements is not an allegation that the US SEC and other regulatory authorities take lightly. There is now a renewed call for more regulation to resolve this alleged lack of transparency and hold those underwriters accountable. Proponents of regulation cannot divorce themselves from calling for more regulation; this is fine. But, once again, credit needs to be given to the current regulatory environment, including the media as a regulator, for its immediate investigation.

This is not an argument against regulation. Regulation is needed and is crucial in the quest for more integrity in business. However, regulation is meant to make the

---

6   *Brian Roffe Profit Sharing Plan et. al. v. Facebook, Inc et al.*, US District Court, Southern District of New York, No. 12-04081.

system fair and free from potential weaknesses and loopholes that lead to corrupt behavior, not for risk-takers who, as a normal part of trading practices, anticipated higher rewards. Over-regulation jeopardizes the economic and social benefits that globalization brings to the world's economy. New risks emerge as the financial system evolves. Facebook, Inc. serves as a case in point to the evolution of the market system because it is a company with a product that is difficult to value using traditional methods. Urs Rohner, chairman at Credit Suisse, captured the markets view of Facebook, Inc., stating, 'I am sceptical of how it [Facebook] can work as an advertising platform. And I believe this explains why the market is uncertain about its valuation.'[7] If Facebook, Inc. demonstrates it can grow revenue, than there is unlimited potential and opportunity in its product. The market is looking for stability and it is about consistent revenue and strong corporate values that treasures transparency, accountability and a good reputation.

DEVELOPING INTEGRITY IN DEVELOPED MARKETS: LESSONS LEARNED

The lesson learned from corruption in developed markets is that a sound business strategy includes the fundamental elements of integrity. A business strategy that divides its culture of accountability, transparency and reputation from its economic targets is susceptible to disruptions without long-term solutions. Every incident of fraud, corruption or failed financial risks today is scrutinized as is used as an example of moral degeneracy. These disruptions cause instability, mismanagement and corruption and can occur despite having a set of rules and regulations to prevent them. Facilitating a business strategy that infuses the elements of integrity as a normal part of doing business is significant because it does not allow professionals to wilfully ignore the standards of business conduct. Building integrity is not limited to providing a proactive platform for your professionals to prevent corruption through awareness and training, but also through the implementation of mechanisms that produces transparency, one of the fundamental elements to promoting integrity in business. Transparency is a self-regulating mechanism for companies. It helps companies and professionals police themselves. Transparency, at its most immediate level, drives professionals to comply with rules and regulations and develop a culture of accountability. It also ensures that professionals are complying with local, national, international rules and regulations. Regardless of your company's depth and breadth in the market, transparency is key to protecting your company's reputation and ensuring it is built on integrity.

---

7   Carolin Schober. 'Facebook IPO Bad Sign for Others: Banker.' *CNBC Technology.* Zurich. 1 June 2012.

Companies in developed markets have been forced to make rather swift and massive adjustments as a result of corruption and failed risky bets. Over a short time, the focus on prevention and immediate responses to corruption has become poignant. The global economy grew and is transitioning at a fast pace. As recent events have demonstrated, gathering information, analyzing and providing cogent reports about companies and their professionals, products or services is becoming part of the most important aspects of every companies' business strategy in both markets. That is, professionals have to know who they are conducting business with prior to any engagement and determine whether or not they are what they deem themselves to beyond financial reports. This is time consuming, but prevents a greater problem; damage to a company's reputation.

Having this knowledge will prevent a company from becoming involved in or a victim of financial fraud, money laundering, Ponzi schemes and other potential acts of corruption. Discovering potentially damaging details about a potential transaction avoids costly lawsuits. Today, with the media's instantaneous reporting, and overall increased transparency, companies cannot afford negative press, especially if it is caused by something as straightforward as failing to know your conducting business with and/or ignoring potential damaging information. Making risky decisions to save money is a sign of wayward leadership. The most important lesson learned is companies without good leadership have a difficult time reforming their corporate culture and face the largest risks and liabilities. When management values material interests over conducting business with integrity, it leads to company failure.

Besides transparency, a strategy that requires a reputational due diligence on each company and individual you conduct business with, and a strong and unequivocal tone from the top, another lesson learned is the value of a company's professionals. Hiring the right professionals in your company has shown to prevent crises of reputation from happening. Professionals are also a direct reflection of your company's business culture. A culture of corruption where failed decisions are not properly scrutinized guarantees that nothing stands to change, even if more regulation is mandated. While anti-corruption policies are increasingly mandated at every level, a company cannot solely rely on it to safeguard against corrupt business practices. Corruption can be the result of organizational culture. Thus, a good business strategy is based on a culture of accountability, where each professional handles himself or herself with the upmost integrity, including having the ability to report corruption without reprisal.

There are valuable lessons to be learned from recent case of corruption. Companies in developed markets have to protect themselves, especially when conducting business in new and emerging markets. There is no substitute for thorough preparation. Training and internal policy development will give you more opportunities to prepare for future problems. Identifying the company's legal and organizational obligations with respect to compliance and anti-corruption policies are important. A poorly planned or ineffective internal control system may be worse than having no internal control system. No matter how well written your policy is, the mere distribution of guidelines will be insufficient to meet legal and company compliance standards. Therefore, training and periodic reminders to all in company is certainly helpful and necessary. These lessons learned are not a complete list of the risks companies face today, but they provide a general direction towards fully grasping the complexity of a globalized world in transition. Only because developed markets have companies that are more stabilized and regulated does not mean problems of corruption do not exist. All markets have to resolve problems of corruption because seemingly minute events lead to larger-scale changes in the global market today. This resolve is attained by emphasizing fair business practices, requiring trust that is not blinded by a lack of transparency, and greater cooperation through compliance towards global ethical standards.

CONCLUSION/NEXT CHAPTER

Business ethics and compliance in today's globalized world should be examined by how it functions in both developed and emerging markets. The differences in business practices and regulatory environments in these markets are so vast that the value of understanding their characteristics is a significant part of companies' business strategies. Prior to today's global processes, these markets were able to function in an isolated vacuum, importing and exporting products via region market systems and/or building relationships across controlled, closed market systems. These business practices functioned without accountability or transparency and were able to accept corruption as a normal course of business. Fortunately, this has changed. Today's globalized world requires you conduct business with integrity. Companies conducting business across several market systems, and within different regulatory systems, have to be more aware of the pitfalls of a bad reputation as a result of a transaction or dealing with questionable characters. Therefore, the success of a company in a globalized world is directly related to how it handles itself across market systems.

This chapter examined business practices in developed markets as well as the critical issues that arise because of divergent, regulatory environments of emerging markets. As the push towards greater global commerce intensifies, ethical business practices and dealing with issues of instability, local corruption, and/or resistance to changes, are inevitable. Developed markets already have strong regulatory authorities that establish ethical market cohesion meant to preserve investor confidence in the market, its companies and professionals. Thus, we have to find solutions within our companies that work together with existing regulations. In response to the problems of fraud and corruption we have faced in the past 10 years, companies are focused on strengthening their compliance programs as a primary solution. The inanity of thinking more regulation can fix what is wrong with the global market system will only ignore the real problem, which is fraud and corruption will continue if companies do not learn from recent cases and incorporate integrity, via a culture of accountability, transparency and limiting risks through strengthened reputational due diligence processes, as the foundation of their business strategies. Chapter 4 examines recent fraud cases and demonstrates how companies and their professionals in both markets require knowledge of how crises happen and how they affect future risks and reputations. Significant regulatory changes and non-governmental monitoring organizations that are in the global fight against corruption have already established successful initiatives. Companies are now charged with aligning their compliance programs with these initiatives or risk more regulation that may impact the advantages of competition.

CHAPTER FOUR

CASE STUDIES OF MAJOR FRAUD AND
CORRUPTION AROUND THE WORLD

There have been a multitude of fraud and corruption scandals of great magnitude that have come to light in the world's media in recent years. The scale or degree of complexity of fraudulent activity and the quantity of money misappropriated and the poor judgement appear to be on the rise. The discovery of fraudulent and/ or corrupt behavior is both a result as well as one of the causes of our current economic state. Regardless, fraud and corruption exist regardless of economic circumstances. In 2010, over 34 per cent of companies reported that they have had at least one instance of fraud or corruption committed against them, a 13 per cent increase from 2009.[1] Furthermore, 1 in 10 of those who reported fraud and corruption 'suffered losses of more than US$5 million'.[2] This is a disproportionate amount of loss when one considers that the average cost of compliance for private firms is $50,000 and public firms report the costs to be approximately $3 million. Fraud prevention costs vary significantly and are based on a company's size, whether private or public. As an example, public companies must adopt corporate governance reforms such as those specified in Sarbanes–Oxley Act of 2002. Whether there are industry-specific compliance codes, and/or whether a company's industry is more susceptible to fraud such as the banking and financial services, government, manufacturing, health care and insurance industries, having a robust compliance program with strong anti-corruption standards and guidelines is more and more essential to safeguarding your business and reputation because fraud and corruption is indiscriminate and the greatest safeguard is preparedness.

The media is saturated with accounts provided by victims, whistle-blowers and admissions of fraud each day. Understandably, the greater the crime, in terms of the amount of money lost, the greater the exposure and public interest. In the most severe cases, reputational damage resulting from fraud and corruption causes the business to fail because of loss of confidence in their corporate structure and system. As this chapter will point out, loose lending standards, incentives to mortgage brokers and other abuses by banking institutions and the industries

1   PricewaterhouseCoopers Global Economic Crime Survey 2011.
2   Ibid.

that surrounded the banking institutions contributed to the banking and mortgage meltdown in 2008, in turn triggering a worldwide financial crisis. This meltdown has led to increased regulation, heightened inspection of the banking and financial services industry, as well as exposure of widespread corruption, and has caused the public to abandon the confidence it once had in the banking industry as a whole. In addition to the loss of confidence, there is resentment against banking and financial services industry. The resentment has manifested itself through social media outlets that have been utilized to mobilize people from both extremes of the political spectrum such as the Tea Party and Occupy Wall Street movements in the United States. As a result, we are struggling to find a solution on how to recover from an economic downturn while we attempt to regain confidence and reconcile resentment towards government for not properly regulating the banking businesses.

This chapter focuses on fraud, bribery and corruption cases that have affected the way our global economy conducts business and how they could have been avoided. From the collapse of Enron and Arthur Anderson to Bernard L. Madoff's Ponzi scheme to the wave of scandals that changed the way business is conducted today, this chapter highlights the many instances where effective regulation and self-policing would have protected stakeholders and the public as a whole. Moreover, this chapter also features examples of how too much regulation by government can suppress the economic engine and inhibit recovery from the meltdown, including driving up the cost of compliance programs. For instance, one of the main criticisms about the US Sarbanes–Oxley Act of 2002 and the US Dodd–Frank Wall Street Reform and Consumer Protection Act of 2010 is that both financial regulatory reforms are time-consuming and expensive to implement, without a clear and compelling cost-benefit case to be made for them. These two Acts are examples of reactionary legislation to reign in corporate fraud and corruption, whereas had there been self-policing, and effective regulation and enforcement of laws already on the books, some of the recent corruption events might have been avoided. Yet, over the past 10 years, the general consensus is that Sarbanes–Oxley has had some impact in the reduction of fraud, misconduct, and other corruption when appropriately implemented. Dodd–Frank is too new to be able to make a compelling case either way.

According to the Association of Certified Fraud Examiners' (ACFE) 2010 Global Fraud Study, 'frauds are much more likely to be detected by tips than by any other method', accounting for 40.2 per cent of initial detections followed by management reviews at 15.4 per cent and internal audits at 13.9 per cent.[3] Furthermore, the ACFE's 2010 Global Fraud Study shows '11 per cent of frauds were detected through channels that lie completely outside of the traditional anti-fraud control

---

3   *Report to the Nations on Occupation Fraud and Abuse: 2010 Global Fraud Study*, Association of Certified Fraud Examiners. 2010.

structure: accident, police notification and confession' and 'the victim organization either had to stumble onto the fraud or be notified of it by a third party in order to detect it'.[4] These are important statistics as governmental legislation, regulatory agency policies, and business policies are beginning to become more amenable to whistle-blower programs that can result in discovery of fraud and corruption at a much earlier stage.

SOCIAL MEDIA AND TRANSPARENCY

Social media, blogs and related media technology have also increased transparency throughout the world, exposing corruption, graft and similar unethical business practices. Computer systems have allowed for movements of suspect money to be traced much more simply, although legal systems have not been able to adapt as quickly to multi-jurisdictional enforcement issues. Yet, media technologies are an effective tool in shaping legal and organizational changes because it has power over the way issues are regarded by governments and the public. However, exposing corruption is not enough to prevent it if governmental actions are weak, accountability is ignored, education and training programs regarding anti-corruption policies do not exist, and there is resistance to change in the way companies conduct business.

The following case studies demonstrate how some businesses have failed while others have been able to manage and live through a crisis despite damage to their reputations and a multitude of penalties. Properly policing your business prevents expensive litigation and overly broad governmental legislation, but should not be the only recourse to action. These cases involve an array of fraud and other criminal behaviors and highlight the issue of transparency. Moreover, they each demonstrate how the corrupt leadership of one business causes a domino effect on other businesses (even if there's no wrongdoing); that is, when a business is shown to be fraudulent, the impact is far greater than the business and actors involved. The impact includes all the businesses within the sphere of influence of the wrongdoers and then ultimately the general public. In analyzing these cases, the same issues appear as a result of the corrupt practices: perceived need for increased regulations, a demand for more transparency, and, most importantly, the loss of confidence in the system. A thoroughly working checks and balances systems among government, media and organizations that are in a global fight against corruption will help investors and the public regain trust, respect and confidence in the global economic system. Also, in the case of Enron and WorldCom, merely allowing the companies to fail is also a solution to the corruption problem, even if the impact to the employees and general public appears to be of great significance. There exists a moral hazard conundrum between government and the greater good

---

4   Ibid., p. 16.

of the impact of global companies within the borders of the regulating country and the global economy. When the Federal Reserve declined to bail out Lehman Brothers, almost immediate negative impact it generated on global financial markets forced an abrupt about-face with regards to the remaining large banks in the form of bailout mechanisms (i.e. TARP),[5] giving a real-life demonstration of the way one firm's crisis can have a global impact. Just the same, the idea that the government will bail out a company no matter how irresponsible their actions are can lead to even more lax behavior in the marketplace.

The Enron Corporation scandal, Madoff's Ponzi scheme, the Mortgage Fallout of 2008, Siemen AG's 2007 bribery investigations, R. Allen Stanford's $7 billion Ponzi scheme, Banco PanAmericano and other cases of fraud and corruption have all had an indelible effect on the public's trust in corporations and in their government's ability to regulate their actions (see Table 4.1). They have led to new legislation, in many cases to placate public anger, whose effectiveness remains to be seen. Legislating ethical practices is simply not enough to restore public trust, and generating enormous costs of compliance only makes sense it they are effective.

ENRON CORPORATION SCANDAL

The largest corporate bankruptcy in United States history at the time represented not only the failure of a company that had at one time been considered cutting edge and innovative, but the failure of regulatory supervision, audit controls and was an indictment of the lack of control and understanding of increasingly sophisticated operations of capital markets. It led to the failure of not only Enron itself, but also what was at the time considered the maximum expression of the 'white glove' accounting firms, Arthur Andersen. It created a domino effect and caused other companies to fail, people to lose their jobs and pensions, and widespread regulatory changes resulting in Sarbanes–Oxley Act 2002. The actions of a few very senior professionals in the firm, together with a small number of third parties, allowed for billions of dollars to be lost and hidden over a period of years. It is a testament to the interconnectedness and fragility of the market system.[6]

The answer is simple in hindsight: the Enron Corporation scandal was not as simple as a bankruptcy filing. In fact, there were indications of fraud and corruption prior to the United States Securities and Exchange Commission's (SEC's) 2001 inquiry

---

5   The Troubled Asset Relief Program (TARP) is a programme under the Emergency Economic Stabilization Act of 2008 in response to the subprime mortgage crisis.

6   In 2001, Enron was the largest corporate bankruptcy (Chapter 11) in United States history, but has since been surpassed by WorldCom in 2002, Lehman Brothers and Washington Mutual in 2008.

Table 4.1   Major fraud and corruption scandals discovered since 2000

2001	Enron Corporation Scandal	Accounting Fraud: reporting false revenue
2001	Arthur Andersen	Accounting fraud in their handling of the Enron audits
2002	WorldCom	Accounting fraud; reporting false revenue
2002	Adelphia	Securities violations; executive theft. Defrauded shareholders of over $100 million
2002	Tyco International Ltd	Executive theft: former chairman and CEO Dennis Kozlowski and CFO Mark H. Swartz defrauded shareholders of over $150 million
2003	Parmalat SpA	Accounting and mutual fund fraud, money laundering
2006	Hewlett-Packard	Spy scandal; pretexting, conspiracy and identity theft
2008	Mortgage Fallout of 2008	Lowered lending standards and provided higher-risk mortgage products
2008	Bernard L. Madoff	Bernard L. Madoff Investment Securities LLC Ponzi Scheme; defrauded investors of over $50 billion. The largest Ponzi scheme in US history to date
2008	Siemens AG Scandal	Bribery and corruption scandals including Siemens AG and Greek government officials during the 2004 Summer Olympics
2009	Robert Allen Stanford	Robert Allen Stanford/Stanford Financial Group Ponzi scheme. Defrauded investors of over $7 billion over a 20-year period
2010	Banco PanAmericano	Accounting fraud; reporting false revenue
2011	Keith Rupert Murdoch	Alleged phone-hacking, bribery and corruption

and investigation into Enron's accounting practices with its partnerships that were used to mask Enron's losses as well as reports by financial analysts who expressed concern about Enron's debt, even after selling key operations and becoming less diversified. Aside from Enron's founder and former CEO Kenneth Lay's history of business failures, indiscretions and necessity to sell off valuable operations while surreptitiously creating new partnerships to hide Enron Corporation's debt, there were other dubious instances that could have provided insight into the company's growing debt. As early as 1987, the discovery of fraud and money laundering by one of Enron's partnerships, Enron Oil Trading and Transport, led to Lou Borget's conviction, costing Enron shareholders over $64 million. Furthermore, by 2001, even Arthur Andersen auditors and Enron's lawyer, Jordan Mintz, questioned, albeit not publicly, Enron's partnerships. The problem was that no one continued to ask questions about these misleading partnerships as Kenneth Lay and Jeffery Skilling, president and COO of Enron, continued to file fraudulent paperwork with the US SEC, publicly claimed that there should be no concern over accounting, trade or reserve issues. Enron was named by *Fortune Magazine* as the 'Most Innovative Company' in the United States on 6 February 2001, despite publishing an article titled 'Is Enron Overpriced?' less than a month later on 5 March.[7] Still, Enron furnished its top executives with multi-million dollar bonuses and continued to fly under regulator and media radar.

Enron is an example of how the perpetration of fraud at the very top of the company made it extremely difficult for anyone to detect and report it until billions of dollars of shareholder value had been lost. There was no culture of compliance and no tone from the top against these practices, since in effect they were being directed at that level. It is also a case of clearly ineffectual regulatory agencies that were not equipped to determine the difference between honest income and inflated, fraudulent, and/or non-existent assets and profits in financial statements. Finally, it represents a failure of Enron's auditors to properly ascertain the risk involved in the company's off-book operations, probably through the collusion of senior professionals at the firm.

In order to analyze what occurred, first we have to understand what motivated Enron officials to institute a system that fudged financial statements and created partnerships to hide losses. Second, why did regulatory agencies fail to discover the corruption? And, finally, how did these deceptive activities by and large escape the financial market's media landscape? The first of many problems with Enron Corporation is that it started as a highly diversified energy company to a less diversified company once CEO Kenneth Lay began to sell off key, profitable assets like Northern Petrochemical, PEAK Antifreeze, and EVAL resins and brought in partnerships like Enron Oil Trading and Transport, Enron Exploration, and Enron ConGeneration, Transwestern Pipeline, and Northern Border Pipeline

---

7   Bethany McLean, 'Is ENRON Overpriced?' *Fortune Magazine*. 5 March 2001.

to hide its debts from its financial statements. The second of these problems, and key to its motivation, is a deregulated energy market that was exploited by CFO Andrew Fastow, COO/CEO Jeff Skilling, and CEO Kenneth Lay to establish limited liability special purpose entities, or partnerships, that permitted Enron Corporation to transfer liabilities to these accounts to increase stock prices and keep its investment grade credit ratings. In fact, it was CFO Andrew Fastow, who created LJM in 1999, a shell company that conducted business with Enron, to purposely hide debt and inflate profits and increase its stock prices. On 5 February 2001, Arthur Andersen probed Enron about its LJM partnerships, but quickly declared there should be no reservations over the partnerships to Enron's audit committee. It was, as we now know, the first of many big lies that systematically operated under the noses of regulators, media, shareholders, investors and the public. While the motivation was greed, Enron's management was also operating in a deregulated market without the stiff mandates of accounting laws stipulated in the Sarbanes–Oxley Act of 2002. This does not justify the widespread fraud and corruption, but it does shed light on how individuals and companies will continually find loopholes in an effort to gain an advantage, even if unfair, over their competitors while increasing their fortunes.

A general theme about major corporate frauds is that the end usually comes in conjunction with a market downturn. When the market is continually rising, it is much more simple to hide fraud. When a downturn occurs it becomes much more difficult. Enron was no different. On 14 August 2001, Jeffrey Skilling resigned as CEO of Enron Corporation for 'personal reasons' after six months in the position. The next day, Sherron Watkins, Vice President of Enron's Corporate Development practice, sent Kenneth Lay, who regained the position of CEO as a result of Skilling's resignation, a one-page letter claiming that Enron's accounting practices were misleading. Sherron Watkins, after alerting former co-workers at Arthur Andersen about her findings, meets Kenneth Lay and delivered a seven-page letter detailing the fraud a week later. Interestingly, between 15 August and his meeting with Sherron Watkins on 22 August, Kenneth Lay exercised 93,620 share options at a total value of $1,998,477.00 and Jeffrey Skilling sold 500,000 of his Enron Corporation shares on 17 September 2001. During this time, Vinson & Elkins, Enron's attorneys, report that Arthur Andersen approved of Enron's accounting procedures and no wrongdoing was discovered while Arthur Andersen hired attorneys, Davis Polk & Wardwell Law Firm, to prepare a defense for itself. By 16 October 2001, Enron announced a third quarter loss of $618 million, a week prior to the US SEC's inquiry into Enron's accounting procedures with Arthur Andersen and its partnerships. It only took 9 days for the US SEC to announce a formal investigation into Enron's business practices. One of the many lessons that we can extract from the Enron scandal is that even a complex, institutionalized and systematic fraud ring involved a few individuals in two companies can be exposed in a matter of weeks and an entire industry and business community will suffer the effects for years by way of expensive litigation, mandated compliance programs, and the dissolution of businesses.

The Enron Corporation scandal quickly became a lesson for investors who overlook the importance of proper due diligence processes, regulatory agencies that disregard evidence of fraudulent history or fail to be proactive against criminal behavior, auditors who do not follow basic risk management practices and the media's inability to grab hold of the story and investigate it further. It is also a cautionary tale about complex financial products that evolve in unregulated or lightly regulated environments.

The Enron fraud ultimately culminated in the dissolution of Arthur Anderson, the accounting firm that was forced to surrender its licences to practice after being charged criminally relating to its handling of the Enron audits, and was also a major blow to the confidence we have in corporations, government and media. Since this scandal, there has been an increase in legislation focused on preventing fraud and corruption and regulatory changes to increase disclosure and transparency.[8] However, since 2001, we have experienced a multitude of fraud and corrupt business practices despite regulatory changes that increase transparency and mandate due diligence processes, increased monitoring by non-governmental organizations that are in a global fight against corruption, and calls for companies to police themselves diligently. Since 2001, when Enron was the largest corporate bankruptcy case, there have been three Chapter 11 filings that have supplanted Enron as the largest corporate bankruptcy case in United States history, WorldCom in 2002 and Lehman Brothers and Washington Mutual in 2008.

PARMALAT SPA

All fraud has an effect on the larger story of corruption and public confidence. While the effects of several acts of fraud and corruption are sometimes and at best restricted to a few, many can have a greater, global effect on shareholders, investors, employees and countries and their institutions. Parmalat SpA, founded in 1961 by Calisto Tanzi, became a multinational corporation in the 1980s and achieved a global presence that was valued at over €3.7 billion by 2002. Tanzi's Parmalat SpA, which specialized in producing milk, dairy and juice products globally, went bankrupt and collapsed as a result of financial fraud in 2003, having been found to be over $12.8 billion in debt. Parmalat SpA employed over 36,000 people in 30 countries in Europe, North America, South America, South Africa, Australia, and China with over 140 production and distribution centers. Parmalat SpA's bankruptcy obviously affected a wide array of people, industries and markets

---

8   These regulatory changes and legislation are discussed in Chapter 5: Drivers of Current Behavior.

across the globe. In a globalized world, individuals and companies, especially multinational corporations that conduct business across national boundaries, are at a higher risk of becoming victims of fraud and corruption by a few. Parmalat SpA's financial fraud and subsequent bankruptcy not only affected its production, distribution centers, and its workforce, but also put a strain on its bank, Bank of America, subsidiaries throughout Europe, Brazil and the United States, as well as the sponsorships it held in Formula One, Racing, ParmaTour, a tourism enterprise, Odean TV, and Parma A.C, a prominent football club, to name a few. Similar to the Mortgage Fallout of 2008 that caused the US federal government to bailout its banking system, the public was stunned that such an established and seemingly successful business could be brought down quickly by fraudulent accounting practices. Today, Parmalat SpA operates with less than half the manufacturing and distribution centers and workforce it once had prior to its bankruptcy. Lactalis, a multinational corporation that specializes in the production of dairy products subsequently acquired it.

Parmalat SpA, once a successful multinational corporation, attempted to conceal its losses after many acquisitions in the late 1990s. It sold itself credit-linked notes (CLN) and bet on its own credit worthiness. In fact, like the Mortgage Fallout of 2008 when Lehman Brothers and other companies that no longer exist, Parmalat SpA sold CLN's to its investors as low-risk products and collateral for loans and credit facilities. This same arrangement led to the discovery of toxic assets. That is, the credit risks to Parmalat SpA's investors were in fact higher than anticipated. The default risks were not properly controlled or understood due to lack of data transparency, compatibility of accounting and compliance practices, as well as proper due diligence that would have scrutinized the company's credit, market, operational, reputational and overall systemic risks. Chapter 6 of this book examines how all categories of risk, when conducting business in a global platform, must be mitigated to ensure that the failure of one company does not cause insolvency in other companies and industries in a domino effect. The running similarity among all the fraud, bribery and corruption cases we have examined is that, once discovered, they cause individuals, companies, organizations and entire industries to no longer meet their own financial obligation once debts become due even if they were conducting business ethically. Fortunately for Parmalat SpA, the bankruptcy they faced in Italy, called a *commissariamento*, saved the trademark and allowed another multinational corporation, Lactalis, to salvage most of its assets.

MORTGAGE FALLOUT OF 2008 AND THE FINANCIAL CRISIS

No crisis that we will talk about in this book affected more people around the globe than the US Mortgage Fallout of 2008. The vastness of this event truly reached and affected the global economy as domestic and international markets were so interconnected by the world's financial system. Policymakers and regulators who were charged with overseeing the financial system simply did not understand or were not able to promptly the halt excessive borrowing and lowered lending standards by the public, banks and financial services firms. The cause of the mortgage fallout could be imputed to several factors, all which continue to remain controversial. It is normal to want to find the culprit during and after 'unexpected' crises. In the case of the mortgage fallout and subsequent financial crisis, finding the one culprit is unattainable and impractical. There are many reasons why the mortgage system in the United States failed and many more reasons why it resulted in the worst financial crisis since the Great Depression. However, the insidious combination of excessive greed, extremely complex new financial products aimed at injecting enormous amounts of liquidity into the market, conflicts of interest, a lack of rigor with regards to lending standards and proper documentation and controls and an overheated market led to an epic collapse of which the entire world is still trying to climb out. In fact, as early as 2004, the FBI warned of '[r]ampant fraud in the mortgage industry' that a 'booming mortgage market, fueled by low interest rates and soaring home values, has attracted unscrupulous professionals and criminal groups who fraudulent activities could cause multibillion-dollar losses to financial institutions'.[9] These warnings were largely ignored and there seemed to be little accountability, oversight or transparency, at any level.

In simple terms, people were lent money based on fictitious values of their homes, regardless of their creditworthiness that had no possibility of every paying off those loans. This created a vicious cycle that culminated in the collapse of a good number of financial institutions in the US and others around the world. Understanding how financial institutions worked during the subprime market boom provides cues about the culture of the mortgage and banking industry in the early 2000s and how the losses incurred as a result lower lending standards now impacts the ability of financial institutions to lend and, in turn, stalls economic activity.

During the subprime market boom, Countrywide Financial became a nationwide leader in subprime, no document, home-equity lines of credit, and other quick type loans. How did Countrywide Financial impact the market so gravely? Basically, loans were being given so freely across the board, real estate prices jumped, often times over-inflating the local markets (i.e., the impact in the Florida and Las Vegas markets, two of the worst hit in the nation). More loans and loan types on the market were incentives to all of the ancillary real estate services to quickly build up and meet the demand of the real estate boom. Appraisers were often changing the values of properties within days of a previous appraisal, just to get the values to match the requested loan. This in turn caused a 'you better put a contract down now or we will just accept the next person that comes along' type of attitude.

---

9   Terry Freiden. *FBI Warns of Mortgage Fraud 'Epidemic'*. CCN Washington. 17 September 2004.

Insurance companies dropped requirements for homes to meet underwriting guidelines in order to keep up with the demand. For realtors and the real estate industry's ancillary services, it became about volume and if you could not handle the volume, someone else could. Proper risk management and compliance took a back seat to a booming market. Countrywide Financial's and others actions led to a boom in the secondary market for bundling and selling their investments to third party investors. Because there was no strict due diligence in place, the investors who purchased these bundled loans bought incomplete and sloppy loan packages.

Mortgage buyers and lenders were not the sole cause of the mortgage and financial crisis. Financial agreements by financial institutions like mortgage-backed securities (MBS) increased interest in the seemingly booming US housing market because the value of these securities are derived from mortgages and housing prices. During the housing boom, MBS were profitable. However, with housing prices in decline as a result of the average consumer's debt load and the expiration of adjustable-rate mortgages, these same financial institutions began to report significant losses. These losses promoted defaults and losses on other loan types in other areas and exposed the fragility of the economy. It quickly became apparent that the problem of the mortgage crisis was deeper than the subprime and adjustable-rate mortgage loans, but was embedded in wholly unregulated institutions like investment banks and hedge funds that were concealing leverage levels from investors and regulators via off-balance sheet derivatives and securitizations. More simply put, financial institutions took a risk on MBS because they believed the housing market would continue to rise and buyers would continue to make their mortgage payments once their adjustable-rate mortgage loans expired. The opposite happened and the assets became toxic and largely worthless.

The first of the large investments banks to show overt signs of trouble as a result of the mortgage fallout was Bear Stearns when, on 10 March 2008, it was rumored in the financial media that Bear Stearns was running out of cash. There was a loss of confidence among investors and Bear Stearns' stock price began to plummet. The social media grabbed hold of this story and, as we know, it has a profound impact on the public's perception, even if it's simply a rumor. Alan Schwartz, former and last CEO of Bear Stearns, attempted to quell the rumors, but it was too late. By 30 March 2008, JP Morgan Chase acquired Bear Stearns, the 85-year-old company that survived the Wall Street Crash of 1929 and the Great Depression without laying off any employees, at $10.00 per share.[10] The Federal Reserve Bank of New York was initially going to 'bailout' Bear Stearns by providing a $25 billion loan, but instead changed the 'bailout' offer to make a $30 billion loan to JP Morgan Chase who would then buy Bear Stearns. As part of the 'bailout' offer, the US Federal Reserve took liability for $29 billion in toxic assets in Bear

---

10    $10.00 per share was a renegotiated price between Bear Stearns and JP Morgan Chase. The initial offer was $2.00 per share (Total: $236 million) on 17 March 2008.

Stearns' portfolio. The risk to the financial system was too great if Bear Stearns was to file for bankruptcy so Ben Bernanke, chairman of the Federal Reserve, was determined to help. The critics of Bernanke's intervention believed it was an issue of 'moral hazard', which is the idea that if you bail someone out of a problem they caused, they will not have an incentive not cause the problem again. However, many believed it was necessary in order to prevent further economic decline. In any case, the Bear Stearns fiasco and its toxic assets, mostly MBS and mortgage-related credit default swaps, seemed like it would be another fleeting moment in the financial industry where one company simply goes belly up. This was certainly not the case as Fannie May and Freddie Mac were placed into conservatorship (i.e., nationalized) of the Federal Housing Finance Agency (FHFA) on 7 September 2008.

By the end of 2008, Wall Street's fourth largest investment bank, Lehman Brothers, went bankrupt. Henry Paulson, Secretary of the Treasury, urged bankers to deal with Lehman Brothers on their own. However, because financial institutions were concerned with their own instability, they wanted nothing to do with Lehman Brothers and its toxic assets. The problem was systemic. As a result, banks stopped lending, the credit markets froze, and the risks and liabilities associated with unregulated financial institutions became a reality. Furthermore, because American International Group, Inc. (AIG), the world's largest insurance company, insured Lehman's billions of dollars in mortgage credit default swaps, it was suffering from its own liquidity crisis. At this point, the idea of 'moral hazard' was no longer an option. Paulson had no choice but to seek capital injection to save AIG from defaulting as well as the banking system. On 14 October 2008, the US government agreed to bail out the financial industry, partially nationalizing it.

Merrill Lynch was sold to Bank of America on 8 September 2008, the same day Lehman Brothers filed for bankruptcy. Bank of America saw this as an opportunity. While this was welcome news for Merrill Lynch shareholders ($29.00 a share) at first, the instability of the financial system was quickly uncovered. Bank of America's CEO, Ken Lewis, wanted out of the deal in December 2008, less than two months after acquiring Merrill Lynch because the losses were greater than expected; Merrill Lynch's toxic assets (i.e., MBS) were going to cost Bank of America more than expected. Merrill Lynch's fire sale price was too good to be true. Prior to the acquiring Merrill Lynch, Bank of America performed its due diligence in 48 hours, under pressure from Henry Paulson to 'save' the investment bank as well as investor confidence in the economy, knowing that Lehman Brothers was filing for bankruptcy. This is not enough time for any due diligence process, let alone for a financial institution like Merrill Lynch. This was the first misstep by Bank of America because a more thorough due diligence process would have uncovered these toxic assets. Bank of America's second misstep was in its failure to fully understand the value of transparency. Merrill Lynch was an investment bank, not a traditional, and therefore more conservative, commercial bank. It took greater risks on investments and assumed significant debts because it was not subject to the same regulations as a commercial bank. Less than a month later, in January 2009, Bank of America's stock dropped by more than 45 per cent and took a $15 billion loss in less than a week.

This shocked the market and caused the power to shift from Wall Street to Washington, DC as federal regulators stepped in and demanded new management, which was authorized as a result of the Emergency Economic Stabilization Act of 2008 that established the Trouble Asset Relief Program (TARP). This bailout, proposed by Treasury Secretary Henry Paulson, authorized the US Secretary of the Treasury to spend up to $700 billion to purchase failing bank assets, mostly MBS, but also gave the government and its regulatory agencies more control over the banking system. Henry Paulson, former Chairman and CEO of Goldman Sachs and proponent of deregulation, was now manager of the United States Emergency Economic Stabilization Fund and oversaw the Financial Stability Oversight Board and TARP (bailout). The Dodd–Frank Wall Street Reform and Consumer Protection Act of 2010 reduced the authorized amount to $475 billion. The mortgage fallout and financial crisis also inadvertently helped expose multibillion-dollar corruption schemes.

BERNARD L. MADOFF'S PONZI SCHEME

There is an age-old adage that if something is too good to be true it probably is too good to be true. Ponzi schemes, which have existed for much of modern recorded history, rely on greed driving people to believe that something that seems too good to be true is actually real. They usually work well until the amount of new victims entering the scheme isn't sufficient to cover the redemptions of others wanting to cash out. A financial crisis is usually a tipping point for a Ponzi scheme, and the larger the scheme the harder it collapses. Thus one can make the argument that the Mortgage Fallout of 2008 and the subsequent financial crisis directly helped expose Bernard 'Bernie' L. Madoff. As a result of the financial crisis, the number of new investors into Bernard L. Madoff Investment Securities LLC slowed while existing investors began asking for redemptions. The financial market, while increasingly complicated and volatile in 2007–2008, still had rules. Therefore, because Madoff's business was a Ponzi scheme, it was exposed by the market's decline. The Lehman Brothers bankruptcy, the conservatorships of Fannie May and Freddy Mac, the fire sale of Bear Stearns and Merrill Lynch, and the US government's bailout of the financial industry on 14 October 2008 provide clues of the market's volatility as well as investor confidence. Despite the down market, Madoff was still supposedly making money and promising unusually high returns. Many experts thought he was 'front running' or using a 'split-strike option strategy'. However, even in both instances, Madoff would have been incapable of getting the same results that his well-managed and contained Ponzi scheme did. Madoff's first advantage was that no one asked questions and when they did, the issue was largely ignored by the US SEC since the 1990s, investors who were yielding high returns on paper, and internal. In hindsight, we now know that there were six failed investigations of Madoff by US SEC examiners since 1992. Madoff's second advantage rested on the fact that he was very well acquainted with the Mary Shapiro, US SEC chairman, and Elisse Walter, US SEC Commissioner. US SEC examiners failed to scrutinize his stock records at the Depository Trust Company, which would have revealed it was a Ponzi scheme according to Madoff. Furthermore, the US SEC neglected financial market media reports that questioned Madoff's investment strategies and had ignored financial analyst and whistle-blower Harry Markopolos' numerous attempts to inform them since 1999. In fact, according to Markopolos, he alerted and sent evidence about the fraud to the US SEC on 'May 2000. October 2001. October, November, and December of 2005. Then again June 2007. And finally April 2008. So five separate SEC submissions.'[11] Madoff's third advantage is that no one did the maths or attempted to duplicate his results to find if his 'investment strategy' was mathematically possible. Markopolos did the math and found that:

> He had the patina of being a respected citizen. One of the most successful businessmen in New York, and certainly, one of the most powerful men on Wall Street. You would never suspect him of fraud. Unless you knew the math ... It took me five minutes to know that it was a fraud. It took me another almost four hours of mathematical modeling to prove that it was a fraud.[12]

Madoff's three advantages were that there was no transparency in his investment strategy, lax or inept regulatory oversight, and credibility and political influence. His $50 billion Ponzi scheme, the largest in history, continued to go unnoticed and, at times, was altogether ignored. When Madoff's employees were asked about the firm's practices and why no one said anything, the common response was 'no one ever asked questions' even when they suspected or found inconsistencies in financial statements that were sent to investors. In fact, it was rare that anyone would ask questions, especially investors, because they were focused on the bottom line and did not want to rock the boat. In retrospect, many of these questions would have demonstrated that it was impossible for Madoff's operation to be legitimately serviced by a three-person firm with only one accountant in Greenwich, Connecticut. There were always suspicions about how his largely isolated business grew; investors and the media simply believed that he was merely protecting his trading strategy. The secret to his business was isolation. Major derivative firms and other Wall Street investment firms did not trade with Madoff because many of their high-ranking executives did not believe he was legitimate. Yet, his fraudulent operation continued under the noses of government, the industry

---

11   Andy Court and Keith Sharman. 'The Man Who Figured Out Madoff's Scheme.' CBSNews. March 2009.
12   Ibid.

and the media until he confided to his sons, Mark and Andrew Madoff, that he was having a difficult time meeting the $7 billion in redemptions and admitted it was 'just one big lie.' His sons reported him to the federal authorities. On 11 December 2008, Bernard 'Bernie' L. Madoff was arrested for running a Ponzi scheme, still the largest Ponzi scheme in United States history. The infamous image of Bernie Madoff arriving at his New York City offices wearing a black baseball cap and trench coat as the media ask questions such as 'How did you pull it off?', 'Do you have anything to say for yourself?', and 'Are you sorry for what you did?' After someone from within the crowd pushed him, Madoff simply uttered, 'Don't push me.'

Bernie Madoff had one caveat that he forewarned his investors and investment advisers about. They were not allowed to list him as their investment adviser in any of their marketing materials because he was not registered with the US SEC, even though he had thousands of clients and handled billions of dollars. Astoundingly, everyone who did business with Madoff operated under this secrecy rule and did not question why he was an unregistered investment adviser with the US SEC. It was simply something that no one talked about. For instance, Madoff circumvented transparency and was able to operate as an unlicensed investment adviser through third parties like Frank Avellino, Michael Bienes and Michael Sullivan, who took on most of the clients after the firm of Avellino & Bienes was investigated by the US SEC for not registering as investment advisers themselves. This firm was charged with unknowingly routing investors into Madoff's scheme. In 1993, the US SEC effectively shut down the firm of Avellino & Bienes. Madoff later claimed he did not know that the firm was operating without a licence and evaded the US SEC. It is still not clear why the US SEC never went forward with a more thorough and aggressive investigation into Madoff's operation.

There were other instances that could have exposed Madoff's scheme. Michael Ocrant, Markopolos' co-worker at Rampart Investment Management in Boston from 1998–2001, questioned Madoff's consistent returns as well. While it did get attention in the media and a meeting with Madoff, he was not able to expose the fraud at the time.[13] On 7 November 2005, Markopolos wrote a remarkable 21-page memo titled 'The World's Largest Hedge Fund is a Fraud' that detailed the Ponzi scheme and sent it to the US SEC. By January 2006, the US SEC prompted a full investigation into Bernard L. Madoff Investment Securities LLC. Harry Markopolos, Michael Ocrant and Frank Casey believed Madoff's Ponzi scheme was going to finally be exposed. However, two years later, the US SEC of cleared Madoff and found no misconduct. Harry Markopolos famously claimed: 'I had

---

13   Harry Markopolos, Frank Casey, and Michael Ocrant. *No One Would Listen: A True Financial Thriller*. John Wiley & Sons. 2010.

given a roadmap and flashlight to find the fraud and they didn't go where I told them [SEC] to go'.[14]

How was it possible that Bernard L. Madoff Investment Securities LLC remained in operation despite investigations into their business practices by the US SEC as well as having received complaints from Harry Markopolos, an independent financial fraud investigator and whistle-blower in Bernie Madoff's scandal, and others for over a decade? Yes, for over a decade there were fingers pointing at the Ponzi scheme, yet the operation kept going. There is a need for transparency in business affairs and, while a due diligence analysis will be able to uncover many facets of an individual and company's legal and financial matters, the media can also play a vital role in uncovering information. In Harry Markopolos' book, *No One Would Listen: A True Financial Thriller*, he emphasizes how he not only provided information to the SEC, but also continually alerted the media regarding Bernard L. Madoff Investments Securities LLC's suspicious business activities because a cursory inspection of Madoff's revenue stream during a volatile market revealed that he was either 'front running', which is buying stock based on knowledge of his clients' orders or operating a Ponzi scheme.[15] As we learned, it was the latter and Madoff was using newer clients' monies to pay off his established clients' redemptions. This case is another example of how lax regulatory oversight, a culture of greed without any focus on transparency and compliance and a management team that doesn't ask questions can perpetrate a fraud that affects millions of lives.

ROBERT ALLEN STANFORD'S PONZI SCHEME

On 6 March 2012, Robert Allen Stanford, chairman and CEO of Stanford Financial Group, was convicted on 13 of 14 counts of orchestrating a Ponzi scheme that defrauded investors of over $7 billion over a 20-year period.[16] The group consisted of Antiguan-based Stanford International Bank (SIB), Houston-based broker-dealer and investment advisers Stanford Group Company (SGC), Stanford Financial Group (SFG) and Stanford Capital Management. Stanford was once considered one of the wealthiest people in the United States with an estimated net worth of over $2 billion. For over 20 years, Stanford advised his investors from over 100 countries that their deposits were securely invested in stocks, bonds and other securities. According to James M. Davis, former CFO for several of Stanford's companies and the prosecution's star witness since 2009, he helped Stanford falsify bank records, annual reports and other documents to conceal the

---

14   The US SEC cleared Bernard L. Madoff Investment Securities LLC in early 2008.

15   Harry Markopolos, Frank Casey and Michael Ocrant. *No One Would Listen: A True Financial Thriller*. John Wiley & Sons. 2010.

16   Stanford was found guilty of all charges save a single count of wire fraud.

fraudulent scheme.[17] Stanford's scheme takes us on an interesting path regarding his power over regulatory agencies, government and media transparency. While this case is still evolving and being prosecuted in both criminal and civil courts, there are a couple of clear points that demonstrate how the fraud was perpetrated and contained. Prior to investigations by the US Security Exchange Commission (US SEC), the FBI, the Florida Office of Financial Regulation and the Financial Industry Regulatory Authority (FINRA), there were indicators that showed SFG's higher-than-market returns were atypical and irregular when compared to the industry as a whole, especially in a bear market. These returns were unusually high when also compared to the rest of the financial industry as it had dealt with the subprime mortgage fallout and the lingering global economic decline. According to the US SEC's press release, Stanford and his related entities:

> ... acting through a network of SGC financial advisers, SIB has sold approximately $8 billion of so-called 'certificates of deposit' to investors by promising improbable and unsubstantiated high interest rates. These rates were supposedly earned through SIB's unique investment strategy, which purportedly allowed the bank to achieve double-digit returns on its investments for the past 15 years.[18]

On 17 February 2009, federal agents raided Stanford Financial Group's offices in Houston, Texas, Memphis, Tennessee, and Tupelo, Mississippi and immediately regarded them as a crime scene and placed the companies under receiverships. By 27 February 2009, the US SEC amended its complaint against Stanford and charged him, Stanford executives, and entities with running a 'massive Ponzi scheme' and alleged that Stanford and Davis had misappropriated over $1.6 billion in investor funds through 'bogus personal loans' that were invested in 'speculative, unprofitable private businesses controlled by Stanford.'[19] On 18 June 2009, Stanford voluntarily surrendered himself to the FBI after obtaining a warrant for his arrest and pleaded not guilty of all charges of fraud, conspiracy and obstruction of justice.

---

17   For his part in the Stanford's Ponzi scheme, as part of a plea deal in 2009, James M. Davis pleaded guilty to three fraud and conspiracy charges. Three other former executives of Stanford's companies are awaiting trial on similar charges as well as a former Antiguan financial regulator who is charged with accepting bribes from Stanford.

18   United States Securities and Exchange Commission press release, *SEC Charges R. Allen Stanford, Stanford International Bank for Multi-Billion Dollar Investment Scheme*. Washington, DC, 17 February 2009.

19   Amended Complaint against R. Allen Stanford and his entities on 27 February 2009 by the US SEC. Stanford was charged with violations of the Securities Act of 1933, the Securities Exchange Act of 1934, the Investment Advisers Act of 1940, and registration provisions of the Investment Company Act of 1940.

There were forewarnings about Stanford's business practices as a professional and his character that should have, in hindsight, triggered an investigation much earlier. After a successful run in Houston real estate in the early 1980s, Robert Allen Stanford started Guardian International Bank in Montserrat in 1985, but moved it to Antigua and renamed it Stanford International Bank as a result of the new restrictions placed on Montserrat's offshore-banking industry. In 1990, Stanford and his wife under-reported their federal taxes by $423,531.36 and currently have tax liens from 2007 and 2008 totalling more than $212 million. In addition, according to 'internal agency records seen by Reuters', US SEC examiners recommended investigations of Stanford and his entities in '1997, 1998, 2002, 2004, and 2005 ... [b]ut year after year, until 2005, their warnings and calls for investigation were ignored by higher-ups'.[20] Despite having warning signs about Stanford's questionable business practices and dubious financial strategy that promised consistently, high interest in a volatile market, regulators largely passed over on an opportunity to save investors billions. Finally, media transparency, at least on the island of Antigua, was non-existent. While Stanford was able to remain under regulators' radars, likely by keeping US SEC's enforcement division veterans like Thomas Sjoblom and Spencer C. Barasch at arm's length, he was also able to somewhat control the media in Antigua because he did, after all, own two newspaper businesses in Antigua and Barbuda and Saint Kitts and Nevis.[21] At this time, the findings of this case are still evolving, Robert Allen Stanford is awaiting sentencing while his former executives are awaiting their trails set for September 2012, and federal authorities are waiting for a jury to decide if they can seize over $330 million across 30 Stanford-controlled accounts that can be traced back to defrauded investors.

SIEMENS AG

Siemens AG has survived as a company despite having its number of scandals in recent years. How is it that Siemens AG has been able to survive scandals while others completely collapse? It is both in the degree of the scandals as well as admitting to a failure in their internal control system, paying the penalties associated with the scandal, and moving forward with an upgraded internal control

---

20   Murray Waas. 'Insight: How Allen Stanford kept the SEC at Bay.' *Reuters.* 26 January 2012.

21   Thomas Sjoblom is a 20-year veteran of the US SEC's enforcement division who 'is one of the most senior attorneys ever to be investigated for allegedly crossing the line from legal advocacy on behalf of a client to violating the law. He hasn't been charged.' Spencer C. Barasch is former head of the US SEC enforcement division in Fort Worth, Texas who on at least three occasions, overruled requests to investigate Stanford. The US SEC's 'formal investigation began exactly one day after Barasch left the agency'. He has not been charged. Murray Waas. 'Insight: How Allen Stanford kept the SEC at Bay'. *Reuters.* 26 January 2012.

system that shows they have evolved as a result of their experience with fraud and corruption within their ranks. Siemens AG is a multinational conglomerate company with six key divisions in industry, energy, healthcare, equity investments, IT solutions and services, and financial services with a global revenue stream of over €71 billion. It is, by all standards, a truly global company with a presence in almost 200 countries. This presence logically lends itself to more risks, augmented criticism in the media when any form of corruption is found, and stiff penalties. On 15 December 2008, Siemens AG pleaded guilty in the US Federal Court to violating the Foreign Corrupt Practices Act (FCPA) and fined $450 million as well as agreeing to pay a €395 million fine for violating German anti-corruption laws. Since 2006, Siemens AG has paid over $3 billion in penalties, including service providers, attorneys and accountants, to settle bribery scandals.[22] Although Siemens AG has been proactive in strengthening its corporate governance and compliance controls since 2006, it is proving to be a hefty effort, but not impossible. On account of increased competition, especially in emerging markets where bribery and corruption are common, it places companies in a position where they either resort to bribery, illegal payments and other forms of corruption to win international contracts or they lose the bidding war to others that will make these illegal payments and other forms of bribery. This is compounded by the fact that Siemens AG is a very large company so, while it may have a strong internal control system in place as a result of the lessons learned from its previous penalties, it is proving difficult to curb the few corrupt outliers. Its reputation of creating slush funds, bribing foreign officials to gain contracts, and bribing labor representatives to ensure advantageous policies in support of their efforts has not damaged Siemens AG. The primary reason is because Siemens AG has made an effort to reorganize its management through a strong internal control system that emphasizes accountability and transparency.

Siemens AG has been revising its corporate governance and compliance systems since 15 November 2006 when over 30 of its offices were raided on grounds of suspicion on bribery, embezzlement and tax evasion, uncovering many of the world's major corporate bribery scandals. The investigation found that from 1999 to 2006, improper payments were made to several top officials by Siemens AG's executives, including alleged corruption in deals stemming from Siemens AG's contract to provide security systems used for the 2004 Athens Olympics to bribing officials from the Association of Independent Employees, one of its competitor's, IG Metall, largest unions.[23] In 2007, Peter Löscher replaced Klaus Kleinfeld as

---

22   United States Department of Justice. *Siemens AG and Three Subsidiaries Plead Guilty to Foreign Corrupt Practices Act Violations and Agree to Pay $450 Million in Combined Criminal Fines: Coordinated Enforcement Actions by DOJ, SEC, and German Authorities Result in Penalties of $1.6 Billion. www.usdoj.gov*. 08-1105. 15 December 2008.
23   Carter Dougherty. 'Siemens Revokes Appointment after Reviewing Files in Bribery Case'. *New York Times*. 14 December 2007.

Siemens AG's CEO with the goal to ensure 'the highest performance at the highest ethical level' and 'made the reorganization of Siemens and the ethical screening of senior executives his signature priorities' so that its financial controllers 'can keep track of where money has flowed'.[24] Since the stiff penalties and reorganization of Siemens AG's lines of responsibility, executive bribery and corruption has decreased. Siemens AG demonstrates that a few key and critical issues need to be addressed that will allow for a successful internal control system, despite a company's history.

In Siemens AG's case, there was a lack of accountability, a strong compliance program, and transparency among its management that allowed employees to participate in fraudulent behavior. This was primarily due to not having proper lines of responsibility in place. Instead, it had an unprepared management and the company's managers indulged in negotiating contracts with bribes because the focus was on the short-term deal that did not consider the longer-term ramifications of corruption. That is, Siemens AG business culture did not adhere to ethical standards and ignored the implications of failing to abide by the set of legal rules set by the global business community, governmental regulating agencies and global standard organizations to ensure fair competition in the marketplace. In addition, despite Germany's Co-Determination Law, which promotes that a company's supervisory board should include labor representatives, the scandals at Siemens and other German companies (i.e., Volkswagen) exposed the policy as largely ineffective. Notwithstanding, Siemens AG has been able to survive from any financial and reputational damage due to the many scandals that were uncovered between 1999 and 2006. However, the case demonstrates that in a largely decentralized and global company, the application of a robust internal control system should be management's priority. Simply publicizing the need for more integrity and lines of responsibility, as its CEO Peter Löscher stated in 2007, will not ensure a strong ethical culture for effective corporate governance.

BANCO PANAMERICANO SA

Banco PanAmericano operates as a commercial bank that specializes in personal credit, credit cards, payroll lending and lease financing since 1990 when it was authorized as a bank in Brazil. In 2008, Brazil's Central Bank investigated Banco PanAmericano and found that it had 'sold bundled loans to other banks while keeping them recorded as assets' thereby inflating Banco PanAmericano's real assets.[25] According to Brazil's federal police and the Brazilian Central Bank's audit report, both charged with investigating Banco PanAmericano, there were

---

24   Ibid.
25   'Nothing to See Here: The Central Bank Claims Credit for a Banking Bail-out in Brazil'. *The Economist*. Finance and Economics. Sao Paulo. 18 November 2010.

'accounting inconsistencies' in the medium-sized bank's balance sheets. Simply put, Banco Americano would not take the assets off their balance sheet once they sold them to another bank in order to keep profits high; therefore, overstating the total equity of their business. Although Banco PanAmericano is a medium-sized commercial bank, it affected Brazil's largest banks since it had substantial business dealings with them. The largest banks that were affected by Banco PanAmericano's management's artificial assets during this period were Bradesco, Banco do Brasil, Itaú Unibanco, Banrisul, Shahin, and Caixa Economica Federal. According to the Brazil's Central Bank's investigation, these five banks accounted for more than R\$4.7 billion in Banco PanAmericano's loan portfolios instead of the R\$637.7 million it reported to the Central Bank in 2008. In the case of Banco PanAmericano, its management's attempt to inflate its assets ignited a greater scandal in Brazil because it affected all of its banks. Fortunately, according to the governor of Brazil's Central Bank, Henrique Meirelles, 'the central bank found the problem before anyone else' and 'a routine check on Brazil's market for loan assignments found different totals for purchases and sales' and discovered the anomalies in Banco PanAmericano's balance sheets.[26]

Banco PanAmericano's management's fraud scheme shows it is just as important to know how the Brazil's Central Bank, federal authorities and affected banks and their advisers responded to this setback and 'organized a solution that meant investors and depositors lost nothing'.[27] Whether there was a whistle-blower or pure coincidence that the Central Bank decided to probe Brazil's market, it was able to halt further corruption and find a solution via a low-risk bailout funded by the affected banks through a deposit-protection arrangement called the Credit Guarantee Fund as well as funds from Grupo Silvio Santos, Banco PanAmericano's controlling shareholder. Banco PanAmericano's R\$2.5 billion hole in its accounts was quickly resolved and shows to be a great example of how a swift response to fraud, isolating the individual and/or company committing the fraud, and finding a creative solution, without any need to use taxpayer funds for a bailout or causing wider loss of confidence in the banking industry, can work. In addition, the fact that Grupo Silvio Santos had enough assets to put up as collateral, over R\$12 billion and covering 34 businesses, also helped to find a creative solution to a problem that could have been worse and allowed Brazil's emerging market to remain largely unsullied.

KEITH RUPERT MURDOCH (*NEWS OF THE WORLD*) AND HEWLETT-PACKARD SCANDALS

The *News of the World* tabloid and Hewlett-Packard scandals reveal how technology can be used to illegally gain competitive advantages today and access

---

26   Ibid.
27   Ibid.

personal and confidential information. Both scandals have placed their executives and management teams under scrutiny and severe criticism for phone-hacking and pretexting techniques, exposing unethical means to obtain information in a technology-driven business environment. Phone-hacking is the practice of intercepting telephone calls and/or voicemail messages without the consent of the telephone's owner. In the case of *News of the World*, the voicemail messages of prominent public figures, including the British Royal Family, were allegedly intercepted to obtain information. It is a form of surveillance used by UK agencies under the UK Regulation of Investigatory Powers Act of 2000, but it does not grant the media these powers. Therefore, *News of the World* tabloid's phone-hacking was not only an unethical means of obtaining information, but it was also illegal. As I have mentioned, all fraud is part of a larger story of corruption. As a result of this discovery of a culture of corruption at *News of the World*, its parent company, *News Corp*, has been the focus of more allegations regarding its culture of corruption where it is purported that another one of *News Corp*'s subsidiaries, *The Sun*, has cultivated a 'culture of illegal payments' to a 'network of corrupted officials' and that 'there were systems in place at *The Sun* to hide the identity of sources, and evidence to suggest those making the payments realized what they were doing was wrong'.[28] While a full FCPA investigation is unlikely because the payments were 'too small and localized', Murdoch's *News of the World* and *The Sun* tabloids scandals violate the ethics and standards of journalism. Furthermore, because credibility and integrity is journalism's foremost currency, the public's focus, scrutiny, and criticism turned onto the media itself.

While the phone-hacking scandal brought down Murdoch's *News of the World* tabloid and led to the arrests of journalists that took part in the spying techniques, criminal charges and penalties for HP's chairwoman Patricia Dunn were largely dismissed in the HP pretexting scandal. Also, HP's chief ethics officer Kevin Hunsaker and the investigators involved in the HP scandal were dismissed pending completion of 96 hours of community service after they pleaded no contest to California Penal Code wire fraud charges against them in 2007. The legal and reputational ramifications of the HP scandal affected a few executives and investigators who were involved and their resignations and community service penalties were able to keep HP from being brought down completely because they were not producing information for the public like *News of the World*, but rather to reveal who was leaking proprietary information. Pretexting is the practice of methodically crafting a situation to engage and cause an individual or organization to disclose information they would not ordinarily provide through impersonation and a complicated scheme. The person(s) or organization(s) who are the target of pretexting are unaware of the scheme and are often led to believe they are obligated to provide the information. In the case of the HP scandal, investigators

---

28   Dominic Rushe. 'Bribery Allegations Increase Likelihood that Murdoch's Media Outlets will Face Charges in US'. *The Guardian*. 28 February 2012.

were assigned by Patricia Dunn to impersonate HP board members and journalists to obtain phone records to identify the source of leaks that furnished HP's business strategies. George Keyworth, former HP board member, ultimately resigned after being accused of disclosing any confidential information to journalists, an accusation he still denies today. HP continues to be a successful business with new leadership despite this scandal. When compared, both scandals highlight the importance of access to information and what they are willing to do to obtain it even if the techniques they use are illegal and/or unethical. These scandals also highlight how industries are held to different ethical standards.

News Corp, which was the umbrella company of Murdoch's former *News of the World* tabloid, continues to struggle against the damage caused by the phone-hacking scandal with bad publicity and plunging ad revenue. The discovery that *News of the World* tabloid's journalists would frequently listen to the voicemails of top officials, celebrities and the general public to get the latest news brought about an intense debate about ethics in the press and has cost Murdoch's companies irreparable financial and reputational damage. There's a sense, and for a very good reason, that media are held to a higher ethical and moral standard because we rely on the delivery of the information they produce to the public. These comparable cases demonstrate the importance of knowing your company, the products it delivers, and the ethical and moral standards that are set based on your product. In a globalized and technology-driven world, information and access to it are increasing held to a higher standard. While a scandal may seem to be similar (i.e., pretexting versus phone-hacking), there will be different consequences and degrees of public relations damage because the public inevitably holds the media industry to the highest standards. This is not to say that many businesses are immune to lowered ethical standards, but that there is a distinction between those that illegally manipulate information to gain a competitive advantage for their product or trademark protection outside the media industry and the media that are charged with delivering information with integrity. Finally, while the premise of both cases is about illegal access to information and social engineering to gain this access, they provide details of the larger story of corruption; both cases involved the use of bribery, which included kickbacks and illegal payments, as incentives to acquire the information.

CONCLUSION

In a globalized world, the impact of the media is magnified because information is no longer restricted to a particular industry or locale as it can quickly circulate over the radio, television and the Internet in a matter of seconds; thus, because information can be rapidly disseminated in condensed forms via social networking sites and the regular Internet, it is often simplified. In order to prevent corruption, we must first understand it. As this review of the major fraud cases in the past

15 years has demonstrated, there were always clues about fraud and corruption prior to the seminal moment when it was no longer possible for those individuals and/or businesses to conceal their misconduct. In addition, this review also demonstrates the importance of performing your proper due diligence prior to conducting business, even if trust is already established between your business partners. Government and its regulatory agencies' policies regarding due diligence and transparency have evolved and will continue to do so as the brand-new fraud schemes are exposed. All of this has led to a much more highly regulated and scrutinized environment in which every business must have strong internal policies against fraud and corruption.

The results of fraud and corruption have led to increased regulatory agencies, more scrutinizing business practices, more bureaucracy in business, and a stronger focus on ethical behavior. Increased regulation, scrutiny and monitoring have led to integrity in business being necessary for survival. It is also clear, however, that reactions to major fraud and conflicts of interest sometimes lead to bad legislation. For instance, when the Gramm–Leach–Bliley Act (GLB) was enacted on 12 November 1999 and repealed part of the Glass–Steagall Act of 1933, the US government believed it would enhance competition in the financial services industry and would provide a 'prudential framework for ... banks, securities firms, and other financial service providers'.[29] It did not. Instead, it removed many of the barriers among banking, securities and insurance firms that once prohibited them from consolidating their investment, commercial and insurance services under on conglomerated brand. Therefore, it allowed for more risk-taking (i.e., subprime loans, adjustable-rate loans, mortgage-backed securities) that ultimately caused the Mortgage Fallout of 2008 and the current financial crisis due to an overabundance of toxic assets. Lest we forget, the Glass–Steagall Act of 1933 was enacted as a result of the lessons learned regarding the excesses that lead to the Wall Street Crash of 1929 and the Great Depression. There is currently a push to re-enact the Glass–Steagall Act as the Glass–Steagall Restoration Act of 2011.[30]

Accordingly, while some drivers of current behavior are due to legislation, these are forced hard tools to combat the increasing costs fraud and corruption have had on the global economy; with the size, scale, and increase of penalties, changes in the law are needed. Legislation that have established guidelines when conducting business, is causing many businesses to examine and evaluate all of their relationships, including but not limited to the said businesses' agents, vendors,

---

29   The Gramm–Leach–Bliley Act (GLB) is also known as the Financial Services Modernization Act of 1999 and the Citigroup Relief Act.
30   Return to Prudent Banking Act of 2011 (12 April 2011) and The Glass–Steagall Restoration Act of 2011 (7 July 2011) were introduced by Marcy Kaptur (Democrat, Ohio) and Maurice D. Hinchey (Democrat, New York), respectively. The Obama Administration opposes re-enactment.

suppliers, key partners and the market to ensure their business is not linked to individuals and/or companies that are identified as high risk. However, we cannot depend on legislation and regulating agencies alone. There are other drivers of current behavior that are non-governmental and can also ensure transparency and integrity in business.

While this chapter focused on cases of fraud and corruption, the next chapter will focus on the drivers of current behavior; US Foreign Corrupt Practices Act, UK Bribery Act, Sarbanes–Oxley, Dodd–Frank, the Organization of Economic C-operation and Development, and Partners Against Corruption Initiative to name a few. These are governmental, non-governmental, and people-driven initiatives, policies and monitoring organizations that provide insight into the world of corruption. They help us understand the types of fraud that businesses may be vulnerable to like fraud, bribery, insider trading, embezzlement, money laundering, identity theft, and, of course, elaborate Ponzi schemes. Also, they provide us with an understanding of the different sources of fraud and when economic motivations with perceived opportunities like lenient regulations and lack of transparency combine to make fraudsters think they can get away with shifty business. In Chapter 5, we will discuss successful initiatives and how social media, governmental and non-governmental organizations and businesses can work together to form a stronger compliance culture and rebuild confidence in the economic system through innovation, improving education on anti-corruption policies via guidelines set by politically non-partisan organizations and preventing national governments and international businesses from attempting to find solutions through action rather than marketing campaigns. This chapter served as a primer for these solutions. It showed how fraud and corruption by a few have damaged the public's confidence towards the entire business community and government.

CHAPTER FIVE

DRIVERS OF CURRENT BEHAVIOR

Looking around the world today, it is hard to believe that as recently as two decades ago, it was perfectly legal and even tax-deductible to pay a bribe in Germany. In France, as long as the bribe was paid outside French territory, it was also legal. Governments and companies looked at bribes as necessary means to conduct business and to compete in certain markets around the world. The United States began globally enforcing the Foreign Corrupt Practices Act (FCPA) as a way of leveling the playing field for US companies who felt they were at a disadvantage to their European peers in this regard.

What has changed? Why is it a scandal today if Siemens AG pays a bribe when so recently it would have been considered a cost of doing business? Does this mean that companies are more ethical today than they used to be? Do we now have a universal standard which all multinational firms will have to heed?

The market system requires governmental and non-governmental organizations that are global, dynamic, and have a comprehensive standard. The regulatory changes of the past 15 years have had a positive and sweeping effect on the way international business transactions are conducted. Many of these regulatory changes are consequences of technology and globalization. The global economy is more interconnected than ever, as funds are exchanged at a quicker pace, providing a catalyst for fraud. On the one hand, there now appear to be limitless opportunities for financial corruption because there is a belief that there is a lesser risk of being discovered due to the relative anonymity of the Internet. Even though there is an increased temptation to commit fraud as a result of technological changes, other regulatory changes are by-products of the loss of confidence in the national and international market systems. Such other regulatory changes are caused by a weakened global economy where advantages are sought by any means, including the need to provide structure as a solution. Chapter 4 makes clear how recent cases in corruption have led to this loss of confidence and the need for transparency and accountability. On the other hand, the spectacular and publicity surrounding these same cases has forced changes in the way the world's governments, companies and individuals behave. This chapter explains how technology, social media and awareness are converging to instil a common regulatory standard nationally and transnationally. Fortunately, global and regional organizations already exist alongside national legislation, and have proven to provide a solid foundation for regulatory enforcement. The following information in this chapter provides an examination of the organizations that continue to be at the forefront of the global fight against corruption as well as legislation that is necessary to create a more united front against fraud. These organizations and initiatives because of the transnational relationships in the global market have to be politically non-partisan while their primary goal is to infuse a 'zero tolerance' culture against corruption. Moreover, the organizations and initiatives have to be examples to show businesses on how to both police themselves by providing anti-corruption guidelines and by also training them on how to set up internal and external mechanisms to monitor and prevent fraud and corruption.

The success of these organizations is attributed to their willingness to form partnerships based on the same principles and collectively develop initiatives that fight corruption. In fact, these organizations' quantifiable results based on cogent research and reporting offer evidence of how the long-term costs of not properly regulating businesses within your country are greater than the benefits. In short, global organizations not only bring about awareness of the issues, but also provide evidence of how reacting to corruption costs more than preventing it. While evidence and awareness provided by global organizations are important, it is equally important to be reminded that prevention measures should also have roots within the safeguards of a business and each country's legislation. The best mechanism for fraud detection and prevention continues to be a simultaneous push and pull between external and internal sources. In each of the fraud cases discussed in Chapter 4, the drivers of current behavior were flawed. These corrupt companies and/or individual(s) followed the temptation to commit the crime because of a similar belief that the risks of getting caught were indeed low; the organization or individual found a loophole or a lack of internal and/or external checks and balances mechanisms that would have deterred the fraudulent or corrupt behavior in the first place.

Fraud and corruption cases like Enron Corporation, Parmalat SpA's money laundering, Siemen AG's bribery charges in 2007, Bernard L. Madoff's and Robert Allen Stanford's Ponzi schemes, Banco PanAmericano's fraud, and technology-centered fraud cases like the HP Pretexting and Rupert Murdoch's *News of the World* tabloid phone-hacking scandals lead us to conclude that regulation (both self-policing regulation combined with limited governmental regulation) is necessary. Otherwise, not only will corruption increase, but also the scale of the corruption, specifically to the degree it affects the global economy will simply get worse. Without self-policing regulation by multinational corporations, stricter and more reactionary governmental legislation will swiftly encircle the global economy. For instance, while the Mortgage Fallout of 2008 was not necessarily a corruption case, it highlighted the need to scrutinize and reorganize regulatory agencies in the United States, demonstrated the way one economy, especially a developed economy like that of the United States, is interconnected with other economies, and, probably most importantly, emphasized the need for transparency and accountability. In fact, the Mortgage Fallout of 2008 could be seen as a large fraud case because differing components of the real estate industry were not interconnected enough to fight off the various types of fraud that combined to lead to one of the largest mortgage meltdowns ever. Had there been self-policing, industry standards in existence, then appraisal fraud and mortgage application fraud would not have overwhelmed the real estate market in the United States and investors or company executives would have questioned the quickly growing and over-priced real estate market. It is unfortunate that a few individuals, whether they are government officials or private sector professionals, can affect the reputation of the business community and a national economy. As each of the cases evolved, the scandals not only cost investors billions of dollars when the share prices of affected companies collapsed, but also damaged public confidence in national and international securities markets.

Regulatory agencies that are global and/or regional in scope like the Organisation for Economic Cooperation and Development (OECD), Transparency International (TI), the World Economic Forum's Partnering Against Corruption Initiative (PACI), and their partnerships with the Basel Institute and influence on national regulatory agencies and initiatives like the United States Securities and Exchange Commission (US SEC), the Foreign Corrupt Practices Act (FCPA), and the United Kingdom Bribery Act of 2010 are cause for optimism in the global fight against corruption. These agencies and initiatives, together with robust self-policing, bring about confidence in the market (see Table 5.1). Further, these regulatory agencies help to ensure there is more integrity in business through transparency and cooperation on a transnational level. As these agency and legislative partnerships continue to evolve, the business professional and their organization stands to benefit from knowing that unfair advantages are being monitored by both governmental and non-governmental agencies and that any discovery of corruption or fraudulent behavior will be dealt with by issuing penalties, sanctions or by exposing such fraudulent or corrupt behavior. In today's global economy, even a whisper of corrupt behavior has a detrimental effect on how a corporation or entity performs. In any case, the level playing field, anti-corruption organizations and national/ transnational policies that have been established ensure that the actual business advantage remains in a company's superior product and services and not because there was an underhanded and illegal pay-off or other fraudulent action that cuts competition off at the knees. Because of the increased use of the Internet and the direct almost immediate impact by exposure of fraudulent or corrupt actions, it makes sound business sense for every organization to protect its reputation by following self-regulation and good, business-minded governmental regulation.

Table 5.1   Timeline of significant anti-corruption policies and initiatives

1933	US Securities Act	Regulated the offer and sale of securities in the US; required disclosure of all material information to primary market shareholders prior to deciding on an investment
1934	US Securities Exchange Act	Established the US Securities Exchange Commission; regulated the secondary trading market (stocks and bonds). Is the basis of the US's financial market
1940	Investment Company Act; Investment Advisers Act	Regulated mutual funds (company); Regulated investment advisers (advisers)
1971	European Management Forum (EMF)	Renamed World Economic Forum (WEF)
1977	Foreign Corrupt Practices Act (FCPA)	Increased accounting transparency requirements (disclosure) of the US Securities Exchange Act of 1934 and addressed the issue of bribery of foreign officials to secure an advantage to obtain or secure business
1987	World Economic Forum (WEF)	Formerly, European Management Forum (EMF)
1993	Transparency International	Non-governmental organization that monitors and brings about awareness of corporate/ political corruption. Publishes the annual Corruption Perceptions Index (CPI), Global Corruption Report (GCP), and the Bribe Payers Index (BPI)
1998	OECD's Anti-Bribery Convention	International agreement of the OECD that aims to reduce corruption in developing countries to create a fair balance among its member countries in the global business environment
1998	US International Anti-Bribery and Fair Competition Act	Amended the Foreign Corrupt Practices Act of 1977
2001	US Patriot Act	Grants increased power to federal, state, and local law and intelligence-gathering authorities, including but not limited to, wiretaps, business, medical, financial, Internet search and library records

Table 5.1   Timeline of significant anti-corruption policies and initiatives *concluded*

2002	Sarbanes–Oxley Act	Sets new or enhanced accounting standards for US corporate boards, including the enforcement of criminal penalties
2003	United Nations Convention Against Corruption	Sets standards and rules that member countries must apply to strengthen their legal and regulatory agencies. Calls for preventative measures to combat corruption and requires its members to return assets obtained via corrupt means
2004	Partnering Against Corruption Principles and Initiative (PACI)	Global anti-corruption initiative to mitigate risks associated with fraud and corruption
2010	UK Bribery Act	Repealed and replaced all previous statutory and common law provisions in relations to bribery. Allows for confiscation of property (Proceeds of Crime Act of 2002) and removal of directors (Company Directors Disqualification Act of 1986) if a crime of bribery is committed
2010	Dodd–Frank Act	Changed the regulatory structure of the US set by the US Securities Act. Streamlined the regulatory process, increased oversight and promotes transparency. Created the Financial Stability Oversight Council and the Bureau of Consumer Financial Protection

UNITED STATES FOREIGN CORRUPT PRACTICES ACT 1977/1998 AND SARBANES–OXLEY ACT 2002

The United States Foreign Corrupt Practices Act of 1977 (FCPA) is commonly known as the law that set a standard for the fight against corruption, bribery and addressing the importance of accounting transparency. The act mainly consists of the accounting requirements set by the United States Securities Exchange Act of 1934, which is the legislation that established the United States Securities Exchange Commission (US SEC), and updated anti-bribery provisions that were developed as result of US SEC investigations in the 1970s. As a result of these investigations, the US SEC found that bribery of foreign officials to obtain or retain governmental or non-governmental business was prevalent. In fact, over 400 companies admitted to the US SEC during these investigations to illegally providing foreign officials with over $300 million in return for favorable deeds.

It was apparent that anti-bribery provisions had to evolve in order to manage the complexities of the financial markets.

The pace of international business transactions had dramatically changed between 1970 and 1990s and had increased the opportunity for financial corruption. In 1998, the International Anti-Bribery and Fair Competition Act of 1998 amended the FCPA to include the OECD's Anti-Bribery Convention. It was considered the strongest anti-corruption legislation to date because the policy made it illegal for a US citizen, US corporation, as well as a person or corporation working within the US, to bribe a foreign official. There are other factors that play a role in increasing opportunity for financial corruption: that is, a weakened economy, corruption in foreign markets without anti-corruption systems, heightened enforcement in others, and the temptation to fall into the habits of bribery. Most of these factors are influenced by the direct need of the individual or entity to gain some type of competitive edge over others without investing time and effort to building relationships through reputation and good quality of service or goods.

Within a four-year period, the United States had enacted some of the toughest anti-corruption legislation (FCPA, 1998), expanded its authority to regulate financial transactions of US and foreign individuals and corporations (Patriot Act, 2001), and set new standards for US public company boards as well as created the Public Company Accounting Oversight Board (PCAOB), responsible for managing, reviewing, regulating, and, if needed, disciplining accounting firms that audit public companies (Sarbanes–Oxley Act, 2002). This stricter governance was of course met with strong approval and opposition. The decision to amend the FCPA to OECD standards was not as controversial. In fact, the primary controversy of this amendment was whether or not the US would maintain a competitive edge against countries with more lenient anti-corruption legislation. Today, we can argue the FCPA did not lessen the competitive edge and, if so, it is minimal when compared to newer requirements stipulated in the Sarbanes–Oxley Act. The Sarbanes–Oxley Act has been criticized for establishing a highly complex regulatory environment into the US financial market and has, in turn, led to smaller US firms and foreign firms to deregister from the US stock exchanges. Sarbanes–Oxley Act was a reactionary policy to fraudulent and corrupt corporate and accounting scandals by Adelphia, Enron, Tyco International, and WorldCom. The actions of a few corrupt individuals and companies forced the US government to take action. However, as we know, the best compliance programs are products of well thought out actions and reactions to the current situation.

THE ORGANISATION FOR ECONOMIC COOPERATION AND DEVELOPMENT (OECD)

The Organisation for Economic Cooperation and Development (OECD) was founded in 1961 and is an international economic organization with 34 member states dedicated to promoting democracy and ensuring good practices in each member country's domestic and international market economies. Prior to 1961, the OECD was the Organisation for European Economic Cooperation (OEEC); the inclusion of non-European members led to its name change and further focused on the transnational aspect of today's global economy. However, since the OECD's founding, most of its members are high-income, developed economies according to the Human Development Index which comparatively measures life expectancy at birth, literacy rates and standard of living based on gross domestic product per capita to determine whether a country is developed, developing or under-developed. While the formation of the OEEC aimed at providing a framework for the European Economic Community centered on the European Free Trade Area, it also facilitated dialogue on corruption. For instance, the Financial Action Task Force was established in 1989 to monitor and combat money laundering and issued a 1990 report that provided Forty Recommendations for combating money laundering.[1]

As a result of the Forty Recommendations established by the Financial Action Task Force, combating corruption by generating the move towards more transparency in international economic affairs turned out to be one of the OECD's most significant successes over that past 22 years. More specifically, Recommendation Number 5 titled 'Customer Due Diligence and Record-Keeping' provides governments, businesses, non-governmental organizations and the general public with guidelines necessary to reducing corruption by requiring transparency. According to Recommendation Number 5, '[f]inancial institutions should not keep anonymous accounts or accounts in obviously fictitious names'. This recommendation not only focused on the prevention of corruption (specifically, money laundering), but also provides a framework for the Financial Action Task Force's concurrent mission to combat the financing of terrorism via due diligence, record keeping, and reporting of suspicious transactions by further stating that '[f]inancial institutions should undertake customer due diligence measures, including identifying and verifying the identity of their customers, when:

- Establishing business relations;
- Carrying out occasional transactions:
  - Above the applicable designated threshold; or
  - That are wire transfers in the circumstances covered by the Interpretative Note to Special Recommendation VII;

---

1   www.fatf-gafi.org/recommendations/40.

- There is a suspicion of money laundering or terrorist financing; or
- The financial institution has doubts about the veracity or adequacy of previously obtained customer identification data.'

Furthermore, Recommendation Number 5 also provides customer due diligence guidelines to be performed for both low-risk and high-risk customers. While these guidelines can be simplified and/or reduced depending on the financial institution's or business organization's risk matrix, the Financial Action Task Force recommends a complete customer due diligence 'as soon as reasonably practicable following the establishment of the relationship'. The following are the Financial Action Task Force's Customer Due Diligence measures under Recommendation Number 5:

a) Identifying the customer and verifying that customer's identity using reliable, independent source documents, data or information.
b) Identifying the beneficial owner, and taking reasonable measures to verify the identity of the beneficial owner such that the financial institution is satisfied that it knows whom the beneficial owner is. For legal persons and arrangements this should include financial institutions taking reasonable measures to understand the ownership and control structure of the customer.
c) Obtaining information on the purpose and intended nature of the business relationship.
d) Conducting ongoing due diligence on the business relationship and scrutiny of transactions undertaken throughout the course of that relationship to ensure that the transactions being conducted are consistent with the institution's knowledge of the customer, their business and risk profile, including, where necessary, the source of funds.

The Financial Action Task Force's Recommendation Number 5 encourages that any new or existing business relationship that does not comply with the paragraphs above (a. to c.) should not 'open the account, commence business relations or perform the transaction; or should terminate the business relationship; and should consider making a suspicious transaction report in relation to the customer'. These measures, along with the measures of both governmental and non-governmental organizations that seek to combat corruption, are constantly evolving by updating their analytical processes. However, these changes provide hints about the future of business relationships and transactions and the importance of transparency and knowing your customer services. The Financial Action Task Force's list of 'Non-Cooperative Countries or Territories' (NCCTs) combined with the OECD's 'The List of Uncooperative Tax Havens' provides information about those countries that have not made sufficient improvements in regulating their markets or have been deemed non-cooperative in the fight against corruption, money laundering, and/or terrorist financing.

The OECD's focus is to provide a platform committed to democracy and a competitive, non-corrupt market economy for its members with policies designed:

- to achieve the highest sustainable economic growth and employment and a rising standard of living in member countries, while maintaining financial stability, and thus to contribute to the development of the world economy;
- to contribute to sound economic expansion in Member as well as non-member countries in the process of economic development;
- to contribute to the expansion of world trade on a multilateral, non-discriminatory basis in accordance with international obligations.

The OECD and Financial Action Task Force are just one of many prominent organizations that are tackling the global fight against corruption in government and business organizations. Unlike the OECD, however, some of these other organizations have missions that are more specific to a certain cause or course of dealing and draw their analysis and provide results based on the Corruption Perceptions Index, Bribe Payers Index, and results from the Global Corruptions Report developed by Transparency International.

TRANSPARENCY INTERNATIONAL

Transparency International, a non-governmental organization founded in 1993 by a former regional director for the World Bank, Peter Eigen, publishes an annual Corruption Perceptions Index. Since 1995, the Corruption Perceptions Index has provided a comparative listing of worldwide corruption that focuses on monitoring and publishes data and analysis regarding the frequency of corporate and political corruption in each country. More importantly, the data utilized to develop the Corruption Perceptions Index is obtained from surveys of business people across developed and developing nations. This data is used for the purpose of drawing attention to corruption within government. Above all, keeping a balanced assessment of corruption is important to Transparency International's mission.

Along with the annual Corruptions Perception Index, Transparency International has published the Bribe Payers Index and the Global Corruption Report since 1995 and 2001, respectively. The annual Bribe Payers Index utilizes the data obtained to emphasize the frequency of bribes in the business setting by a country's multinational corporations. Using the Corruptions Perceptions Index and the Bribe Payers Index as empirical evidence of corruption, the Global Corruption Report is designed to provide policymakers, media, and the most importantly the public with evidence of and recent developments in business corruption for over 30 countries. The genius of Transparency International's Global Corruption

Report is that it is made accessible to a wide array of readers and provides solutions, guidelines and recommendations within the report to combat corruption both within a country and transnational borders. The Global Corruption Report is available directly via Transparency International's website. Thus, the Global Corruption Report is readily available to anyone who wants to assess the state of corruption within their country or within multinational corporations, in order to ensure that corporations, businesses and even individuals are operating in a corruption free environment. One of the main objectives of the Global Corruption Report is to keep its assessments as objective as possible and reduce subjectivity so that the report has the greatest impact by stopping current corruption and by preventing future corruption. Through the use of statistical data, the impact of the Global Corruption Report has been to expose the fraudulent nature of business.

Transparency International's method in keeping the results of the Global Corruption Report objective is to allow a wide array of collaborators and contributors to partake in the creation of each annual report. Based on the particular sector that the report is focused on each year, Transparency International invites contributors who have different perspectives, opinions and levels of experience to examine the topic that is being scrutinized. Not only does the Global Corruption Report bring corrupt practices to the world's attention, the report also recommends solutions to ending corruption. The Global Corruption Report continues to serve as a tool to help policymakers, businesses and the general public monitor, change and find solutions to corruption by serving as an objective guideline. The Global Corruption Reports results help to implement change whenever corruption or a flaw in the policies or guidelines of nations or a businesses' system or procedure is detected.

Transparency International's success is measured by the organization's role in fostering a worldwide dialogue about how corruption impedes development or thwarts competition. Its success has even shaped the World Bank's and the International Monetary Fund's views on corruption in the past 20 years. Not only has Transparency International influenced the viewpoints and policies of governmental organizations and business professionals, but Transparency International has also facilitated other initiatives like the United Nations Convention against Corruption and the OECD Convention on Combating Bribery of Foreign Public Officials in International Business Transactions (OECD Anti-Bribery Convention). Transparency International has assisted in the development of tools for organizations to build coalitions against corruption with the belief that corruption is not inevitable, nor a standard business practice. Accordingly, Transparency International's website states:

> *Transparency International is the global civil society organization leading the fight against corruption. It brings people together in a powerful worldwide coalition to end the devastating impact of corruption on men, women and*

children around the world. TI's mission is to create change towards a world free of corruption.[2]

What makes Transparency International successful is that it has created a global network of locally established chapters that provides governments, businesses, and the public with dedicated anti-corruption initiatives that are relevant to today's global economy and that are specialized to meet the needs of industry. Furthermore, Transparency International remains a politically non-partisan organization that works well within coalitions and with other organizations such as member companies of the World Economic Forum and the Basel Institute on Governance to develop The Partnering Against Corruption—Principles for Countering Bribery (PACI principles) which were derived from Transparency International's Business Principles for Countering Bribery. Moreover, Transparency International works with developing nations by providing anti-corruption assistance from a neutral point of view. Data that has been collected over the years can be utilized to support positive, healthy and competitive business and governmental environments.

THE WEF'S GLOBAL RISKS REPORT AND PARTNERING AGAINST CORRUPTION INITIATIVE

The European Management Forum was founded by business professor Klaus Schwab in 1971 and later changed its name to the World Economic Forum in 1987. The World Economic Forum is known for its annual invitation-only event, simply referred to as Davos, which draws about 2,500 global political and business elites to discuss and report on the most salient issues the world is facing, including health, education, the environment and corruption. The World Economic Forum produces annual global reports and initiatives in a wide range of issues affecting its members. For the purpose of this discussion, we will focus on the World Economic Forum's PACI and the Global Risks report.[3] The importance of the Global Risk report is how it demonstrates the way risks are globally interconnected, provides an assessment and solution to the risks identified, and offers systematic techniques to mitigate these risks. As the World Economic Forum's states:

We are living in a new world of risk. Globalization, shifting demographics, rapidly accelerating technological change, increased connectivity, economic uncertainty, a growing multiplicity of actors and shifting power structures

---

2   http://www.transparency.org/.

3   The World Economic Forum's Global Risk Report is based on their Global Risk Network's findings. The Global Risk Network was established in 2004 to report on the risks in economics, geopolitics, environment, society, and technology using qualitative and quantitative data.

combine to make operating in this world unprecedentedly complex and challenging for corporations, institutions and states alike.[4]

In Chapter 1, we detailed the benefits of understanding and operating your organization utilizing the Holistic Layered Integrity/Business Ethics Approach. That is, your organization cannot operate in a bubble. It must remain informed about developments that seem to be beyond your immediate scope. The same is true for institutions that are in a global fight against corruption. At this point, we have witnessed how corruption by one person, a few individuals, and/or one or more organizations can cause damage to the reputations of several organizations or an entire industry, including those governmental agencies and non-governmental institutions that are charged with detecting corruption. For this reason, the significance of the Global Risks Report annual publication ahead of the World Economic Forum's meeting in Davos, Switzerland cannot be overlooked because it serves as a truly global platform to call attention to the global 'Risk Landscape' to over 2,500 participants representing over 100 countries, over 1,000 of the world's top companies, global media leaders, academic institutions, religious leaders, heads of state and representatives of non-governmental organizations. The Partnering Against Corruption—Principles for Countering Bribery (PACI principles) and Partnering Against Corruption Initiative Initiative) reinforce the World Economic Forum's commitment to fighting corruption in part by bringing together a very large, diverse group of people whose main goal is to identify and eradicate fraud and corruption.

PRINCIPLES FOR COUNTERING BRIBERY (PACI PRINCIPLES) AND INITIATIVE (PACI INITIATIVE)

The World Economic Forum believes that PACI principles 'will raise standards across industries and contribute to the goals of good governance and economic development'.[5] These principles are prefaced with the PACI principles' 'two fundamental actions—the adoption of a "zero tolerance" policy on bribery and the development of a practical and effective "programme" of internal systems and controls for implementing that policy'. These principles are derived from Transparency International's anti-bribery principles developed in partnership with private sector interests, non-governmental organizations and trade unions.[6] Accordingly, the PACI principles not only provide a framework for 'good business practices and risk management strategies for countering bribery', but also they also

4   http://www.weforum.org/issues/global-risks.
5   'Partnering Against Corruption—Principles for Countering Bribery,' published by World Economic Forum (January 2004).
6   'Business Principles for Countering Bribery,' published by Transparency International and Social Accountability International (December 2002).

provide an adaptable guideline for your specific enterprises' needs to implement the 'fundamental values of integrity, transparency and accountability' in your organization.[7]

The PACI principles contain five sections that focus on defining these principles, developing an effective program, and implementing this program to combat corruption, specifically bribery. The PACI principles text, in Section 2, defines bribery as:

- The offering, promising or giving, as well as demanding or accepting, of any undue advantage, whether directly or indirectly, to or from:
  - A public official;
  - A political candidate, party or party official; or
  - Any private sector employee (including a person who directs or works for a private sector enterprise in any capacity);
- In order to obtain, retain or direct business or to secure any other improper advantage in the conduct of business.[8]

Furthermore, it addresses the issue of implementation of an 'effective programme' that must include a code of ethics, policies and procedures, training and monitoring and updating once the programme is established. Every internal compliance programme must continue to be updated because criminal behavior is constantly evolving. Therefore, the text of the PACI principles also provides a guideline, in Sections 3–5, on how to not only develop your anti-corruption policy, but also administer it. Briefly, Sections 3–5 of the PACI principles are outlined as follows:

Section 3: Development of a programme for countering bribery.

Section 4: The programme: scope and guidelines.

- Bribes; political contributions; charitable contributions and sponsorships; facilitation payments; gifts, hospitality and expenses.

Section 5: Programme implementation requirements.

- Organizations and responsibilities; business relationships; human resources; training; raising concerns and seeking guidance; communication; internal controls and audit; monitoring and review.

---

7   Ibid.
8   'Partnering Against Corruption—Principles for Countering Bribery,' published by World Economic Forum (January 2004).

Each of these sections provides guidance for a company to devise their anti-corruption policy within their respective compliance program. The PACI Principle also harmonizes with the Holistic Layered Business/Integrity Ethics Approach discussed in Chapter 1 whereby each business relationship should be valued equally. In addition, a company's anti-corruption policy must be applied to every transaction and remain consistent. Under Section 5.2 Business Relationships of the PACI principles, business relationships include the following: subsidiaries, joint ventures, agents, advisers and other intermediaries, and contractors, subcontractors and suppliers. These subsections focus on the need to perform your due diligence as part of your anti-corruption policy, often repeating itself to ensure clarity. Furthermore, the PACI principles suggest carrying out the due diligence prior to any appointments, prior to entering joint ventures, and ensure contractors and subcontractors have their own anti-corruption policy and are aware of yours.

The World Economic Forum introduces its Partnering Against Corruption Initiative as 'a global anti-corruption initiative, developed by companies for companies' that serves as 'a risk mitigation platform to help companies:

1. Design and implement effective policies and systems to prevent, detect and address corruption.
2. Benchmark internal practices against global best practice through peer exchange and learning.
3. Level the playing field through collective action with other companies, governments and civil society.'[9]

Most importantly, the PACI Initiative is a collective effort that includes the OECD Convention on Combating Bribery of Foreign Public Officials in International Business Transactions, ICC Rules of Conduct to Combat Extortion and Bribery, the anti-bribery provisions of the revised OECD Guidelines for Multinationals, the Global Compact's 10th Principle, and a myriad of other governmental and private sector initiatives. This ensures, like Transparency International, that the PACI principles and Initiative remains politically non-partisan and no special interest, other than the global fight against corruption, exists. The PACI Initiative represents one of the most effective anti-corruption initiatives ever employed and works to reinforce, not replace, a company's internal compliance efforts.

CONCLUSION

Despite the fact that the current programs, initiatives, and legislation discussed in this chapter has an overall poor track record in reigning in corrupt behavior by companies, individuals and governments, some appreciable progress has been

9   http://www.weforum.org/issues/partnering-against-corruption-initiative.

made and the risks of doing nothing are too great to ignore. As we know from the examples of corruption discussed in Chapter 4, an unregulated stance on business operations will lead to corruption. The purpose of a business is to provide a product and/or service and seek an advantage while following the rules of the field. Lest we forget, rules and standards are needed and should be understood as a benefit; that is, as a tool that prevents you and your company from having a disadvantage as you do business with integrity. What must be emphasized is that conducting business with integrity safeguards your reputation, protects your brand, and makes commercial sense.

The rise of social media is also serving as a regulatory agent. This chapter examined the regulatory environment and its impact based on corruption and fraud. It must be noted that although it seems as if there is more corruption today because of the rise of social media and the ability to receive detailed information from many media channels, corruption has always been present in businesses. While this may seem like an optimistic view of the business environment, it is not. Businesses are no more and no less fraudulent or corrupt than they were in the past. In the past 10 years, a combination of the transparency created by the social media, and its ability to be a regulatory agent in itself, business ethics, self-policing, and governmental regulation all have had an impact on business integrity. In fact, social media has offered the ability for more individuals and organizations to police the integrity of businesses in a virtuous cycle instead of just the governments and/or agencies (see Figure 5.1).

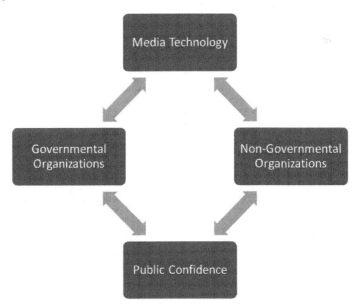

Figure 5.1   The cycle of transparency and access to information

There is a virtuous cycle of social media and other mechanisms for awareness leading to public pressure to transparency leading to government regulations and oversight leading to self-policing mechanisms for businesses. Social media, blogs and related media technology have increased transparency throughout the world, exposing corruption, graft and similar unethical business practices. Computer systems and media applications have allowed for movements of suspect money to be traced much more simply, although legal systems have not been able to adapt as quickly to multi-jurisdictional issues. On the one hand, we must be careful not to over-regulate business operations as this will lead to too much bureaucracy and can stifle business growth and development. On the other hand, there is also a strong argument for regulation based on the existence of corruption. Over-regulated states stand the risk of losing out on contracts to those businesses that do not operate with as much self-policing or governmental regulation. We cannot lose the competitive edge because of regulation. Instead, we need a global standard that positions every business on a level field and allow competition and the best product and/or services to determine a business's success. The impact of a developed nation versus a developing nation's anti-corruption policies can have a dramatic impact on competition, safety and quality of products or services. It is necessary to enforce risk mitigation platforms to help companies police themselves along with ensuring they are compliant with the standards issued by global and regional regulatory programs as well as shareholder expectations.

CHAPTER SIX

WHAT IN THE WORLD IS WRONG?

The idiom 'where there is smoke, there is fire' qualifies as an important caveat to consider when conducting business in a globalized world. When mitigating your risks in a globalized world, the expression also extends to being aware of whom you conduct business with and understanding that your associations impact your reputation. That is, even if you are not involved in fraud and corruption, or did not have any knowledge of it, you and your company's reputation can be in jeopardy if your associations are fraudulent. It is also clear that unfettered greed seems to be at the root of much fraud and corruption, and it remains unchecked by compromised judicial and regulatory systems, leaving the companies themselves to implement the first line of defense. This chapter serves as guide to identifying these risks and ensuring your tangible and intangible assets are properly allocated in a global business market. Those individuals and companies that allocate their assets properly also have the tools to successfully deal with fraud and corruption because they are suitably outfitted to prevent business interruption events. Successful individuals and companies are able to identify those cases of severe or repeated abuse of business practices because prior to any and all of their business engagements, financial, legal, political and reputational risks have been identified by their leadership and compliance programs. They have evaluated these various risks, exposed the risks when necessary, and minimize the risks by developing relevant recommendations based on the lessons learned from fraud and corruption, including terminating transactions and associations as soon as the 'smoke' is identified.

Where there is smoke there's fire, and there was a lot of smoke in the fraud and corruption cases that were examined in the previous chapters. As evidenced in Bernard L. Madoff's Ponzi scheme, many of his defrauded investors who transacted business with Madoff were based on recommendations from other investors who also blindly trusted his operation. A reputational due diligence, which would have easily revealed Madoff's shaky history with the U.S. SEC and his firms unusually stable returns in volatile markets, would have saved investors' assets if they did not incontestably trust these recommendations prior to engaging in business with him; it seems taboo to investigate and perform a reputational due diligence despite the findings that show how many cases of fraud and corruption could have been thwarted by simply knowing your who you are doing business with prior to engagement. Performing a reputational due diligence should not imply distrust. From this perspective, it is as if the individual or company asking for a reputational due diligence is questioning the other's integrity. This is not the case. On the contrary, when you ask for a reputational due diligence prior to engaging in any business, you effectively start your self-regulation instead of relying on government or other non-governmental entities to do that job for you. You are able to identify the many categories of risks that are evaluated during the reputational due diligence process and provide a direction for you and your company to grasp the complexity of the risks involved. History has shown that the consequences of fraud and corruption are disastrous. Moreover, these consequences are often a result of a few individuals who, time and time again, were placed in positions of trust and were able to circumvent company rules and regulations to gain an unfair advantage while placing the liabilities on others, specifically the company's employees, investors, stakeholders and the company's brand and reputation.

WHAT IN THE WORLD IS WRONG?

What is wrong is that the main solutions we have had to this point, regulatory initiatives and legislation, have failed to combat fraud and corruption because they are reactionary policies that do not take into consideration the importance of organizational culture and personal integrity. Before we focus on the solutions that focus on the legal, systemic, technical and market measures that would greatly reduce fraud and corruption, whether in multicultural, trans-jurisdictional or your country's own legal framework, we have to focus on the disputes that arise because of issues that need to be resolved within a company's organizational structure and culture. This means that we have to examine the obvious problem in fraud and corruption cases that is often ignored by those working to resolve the problem, the individual and company culture. Because we are discussing integrity, the individual becomes the most important element of the company and its culture. From leadership to key suppliers and vendors to new employees, integrity needs to exist in the individual in order for it to exist in the company and, in turn, in the global market. Individuals serve as the company's gateway to ethical behavior. This is reflected in the experience of fraud and corruption being perpetrated by one or a few individuals rather than an entire company. Unfortunately, in these same cases, fraud and corruption were able to continue as long as they did because the company itself did not have the internal control system that would have thwarted these few individuals' criminal behavior in the first place. Thus, by simply inserting a command-and-control approach to fraud and corruption, we assume that criminal behaviors will change by enacting and enforcing a law. Surely, this has not deterred fraud and corruption and forces us to question whether or not integrity in business exists.

Does integrity in business exist? The easy answer is that integrity does not exist in business because every company's bottom line is its bottom line. This is partly true. Every company's goal is to improve their bottom line by growing revenue and increasing its efficiency, even if it means making decisions that are not fitting for every individual (i.e., downsizing, layoffs and other cost-cutting measures). These are part of the culture of competitiveness in business and will not change. Every company's leadership needs to make decisions that can negatively impact a person's livelihood. These types of decisions have nothing to do with integrity. Business professionals understand that all companies attempt to improve their performances. What is false is that integrity does not exist in business. This is the more difficult answer because it goes against what we have witnessed in recent years with fraud and corruption. However, the common reaction to any revelation in the financial industry about a loss triggers a call for more regulation, even if fraud and corruption are not present and the loss occurred because of a risky business decision that is part of the nature of the industry. For instance, a $2 billion trading loss by a division of JPMorgan Chase triggered calls for more regulation and 'quickly revived debate about whether banks can be trusted to handle risk on their own'.[1] In addition, this $2 billion loss also triggered reactions in the stock market as 'banks stocks were hammered in Britain and the United States, partly because of fear that the JPMorgan loss would lead to tougher regulation of financial institutions' and this news 'by itself shaved 25 points off the Dow Jones industrial average, which was up about 30 points on the day' because of fears of more regulation.[2] This is yet another case on how a company, even one that has been celebrated as an ethical institution because it survived the financial crisis unscathed, will have to suffer reputational damage even though the type of trade that led to this loss is not banned and completely legal. CEO Jamie Dimon immediately acknowledged JPMorgan Chase's mistakes and asserted that this type of trade, in credit derivatives, was designed to hedge against and minimize financial risks rather than make a profit for the bank. Dimon also believes that this kind of mistake will 'not jeopardize JPMorgan Chase' and will support 'inquiries from regulators'.[3] In the past, this call for more transparency, accountability and acknowledgement of 'bad judgment' would not have been as swift. Today, because reputation has more weight in the global business community, there is an incentive to resolve the issue quickly and rebuild public confidence in your company.

---

1   Daniel Wagner. 'JP Morgan Loss Sets off Call for Heavier Regulation.' Associated Press. Washington, DC. 7 May 2012.

2   Ibid. This news also caused shares of Barclays, Royal Bank of Scotland, Goldman Sachs, and Morgan Stanley to decline by at least 2%, and Citigroup by 4%, because 'because of regulatory fear, not because there was reason to believe other banks would discover similar losses'.

3   MTP Transcript for 13 May 2012. Jamie Dimon. MSNBC.com and News Services.

Regulations have not prevented a few individuals and companies from overstepping ethical boundaries. The more difficult answer to comprehend is that integrity and ethical behavior in the global business community is becoming incentivized. That is, integrity exists in business not only because of stricter regulations that require transparency and curb corrupt practices, but also because business professionals and companies understand that reputation in a globalized world affects your bottom line. The system is regulating itself due to the intensification of the social media and the ability to communicate faster, and with a wider audience, in a globalized world. The command-and-control approach to fraud and corruption is popular because it targets specific actions and appears to be the simplest solution to combating criminal behavior. However, this approach has its limitations and does not address other considerations such as how too much regulation puts restraints on competitiveness, how standard policies are often not tailored to individual, company, and/or industry needs and are therefore deemed inefficient, and imposes superfluous measures on companies and industries that have operated with integrity and their only fault was taking a completely legal risk. Rather than this one-size-fits-all approach to combating fraud, which does not have an efficient record of combating fraud and corruption, the alternative is to encourage companies and industries to find a balance within their company's business culture and show how improved performance relies on conducting business with integrity. Because companies are focused on their bottom lines, this is an incentive-based strategy that will force companies to challenge fraud and corruption, focus on ways to ensure more ethical behavior, build a culture of accountability, and value integrity.

There are many examples of individuals and companies that mediate competitiveness with integrity and demonstrate that you do not have to compromise your values to be a successful company and/or remain competitive in the marketplace. Beyond innumerable endeavors in philanthropy that details integrity with regards to social responsibilities, most companies today are mindful that part of improving its performance and bottom line numbers is ensuring the possibility of fraud and corruption is eliminated from their ranks. Whether a company has experienced fraud and corruption or is seeking to prevent it based on others' experiences, self-reporting fraud and corruption, increased transparency, and a more scrutinizing due diligence process are fast becoming integral parts of fraud prevention programs, especially when conducting business trans-jurisdictionally. Companies are also more focused on *learning* how to deal with fraud and corruption based on these experiences. Companies and their professionals are becoming aware that having robust, internal compliance programs are not only good for their own company, but also enhances the global business community as a whole. That is, compliance programs are attached and inevitably affect each other in a globalized world. Therefore, cooperation and the ability to organize them in such a way that there is an expectation of integrity and fair business practices among your peers is important to combating fraud and corruption. The business community already understands that, if not abated, fraud and corruption could compromise and damage their reputations and jeopardize their businesses, employees' livelihoods, and the global economy. This is an incentive in itself.

The general reputation of business people, specifically because of the saliency of fraud and corruption cases in the media, has clearly caused damaged. In fact, these cases have not only produced a view of business and integrity as oxymoronic, but the idea of a business that operates with integrity is met with a perceived impossibility, especially in businesses that operate in multicultural and trans-jurisdictional settings. Moreover, when debating whether or not integrity exists in business, the public and private discourse is encased with pejoratives. For years, even before the Mortgage Fallout of 2008 that led to the bailout of the US banking system and the recession, 'Wall Street' has become synonymous with greed, fraud and corruption. It has been redefined as a direct derogatory remark with a disparaging meaning towards every business and is constantly reemphasized in the media after another case of fraud and corruption is unveiled. This produces the type of thinking that is limiting and creates a conflict. It leads to calls for more regulation although history shows that more regulations have not deterred individuals from finding new ways to gain unfair advantages against their competitors. What more regulation provides is a short-term solution that penalizes the entire business community as a result of the actions of a few; it also allows politicians, regulators and the media to call for more transparency and integrity in business, but without practical ideas on how to achieve them. These calls for more transparency and integrity rely on the idea that these goals are reachable through legislation and harsher penalties when, in fact, the only serve to further tarnish the image of business professionals, companies and industries. Over the past 10 years, after each experience of fraud and corruption, there have been efforts by the business community to regulate itself by adopting stronger compliance programs and allocating more company resources to ensure accountability. This is based on the awareness that all businesses need to hold themselves accountable to higher standards and that self-regulation, as well as public confidence, should be earned rather than demanded.

FIXING WHAT IS WRONG IN THE WORLD

How does the global business community strike a balance between having a strategy that prevents fraud and corruption while remaining competitive in all markets? In Chapter 4, I provided a detailed diagnostic of how these problems occurred. This chapter focuses on the 'lessons learned' from these experiences and provides recommendations and concrete solutions that emphasize the importance of company and/or an industry's business culture. To this point, we have not been creative in fixing what is wrong with the world. The driving force behind an effective regulatory system and fighting corruption is not repeatedly doing that which has already been done: more regulatory policies, more penalties, and more reforms that interrupt competition and further damage the reputation of the business community. As Chapter 5 shows, the increase in legislative policies and international initiatives have positively helped shaped today's regulatory environment because external controls are needed. However, these policies and initiatives seem duplicative, requiring more transparency via more reporting while administering more severe penalties, and have not fully deterred fraud and corruption. In fact, the only difference is in their promise to implement existing policies and initiatives with greater force, covering every corner of the globe. Fixing what is wrong in the world requires us to understand that while the oldest problem in business is greed, leading to fraud and corruption, it is feasible to reach a balance between external and internal controls to achieve integrity without having to compromise competitiveness.

In Chapter 1, I assessed that a holistic layered business integrity/ethics approach to conducting business is the optimal solution to achieving transparency and integrity in your business. This simply means that you know your company, its employees, key partners and suppliers, clients and markets prior to engaging in business by performing a reputational due diligence on your associations and hiring qualified individuals in your company. It also means there are standards, both external and internal, that guarantee clarity in the expectations and professionalism in the company. These standards will be the defining qualities of your business that attach specific ethical expectations on your leadership, professional associations and each employee in your company. What a holistic layered business integrity/ ethics approach offers is a relationship between external regulatory requirements and internal ethical codes and guarantees every individual and company associated with your company the confidence that your products and/or services are provided with minimal risks to their assets, reputations and own integrity. More importantly, it fosters a culture of accountability. Conducting business with integrity also requires a constant review of your company's risks and ensuring your assets are properly allocated.

The risks to your assets must always be under evaluation as if in crisis mode. Your company needs a long-term and practical strategy designed to limit risks and protect your assets. Under a holistic layered business integrity/ethics approach, the potential risks to your assets are constantly analyzed and your strategy for performance improvement relies on having established protocols to deal with problems of fraud and corruption as they arise. While some of these problems may be unpredictable, such as taking a risk on an investment, fraud and corruption within your company can be anticipated and planned for accordingly. This means that your company must be able to adapt and resolve inconsistencies quickly. It is how your company deals with fraud and corruption that will determine the outcome. Because you are well prepared with knowledge of your employees and professional associations, as well as external and internal ethical requirements, your ability to identify and/or resolve potential risks will also be layered in that solutions to both predictable and unpredictable problems will have a sense of order and allows for seamless continuity in business. Finally, this approach provides your company and employees an internal mechanism of accountability whereby everyone operates with a philosophy of transparency, accountability and cooperation.

Below is an examination of how companies and individuals can minimize their risks by properly allocating their assets. This discussion will begin by exploring what is asset allocation and how it is important in a globalized world where you are increasingly conducting business in a multicultural and trans-jurisdictional environment. This will be followed by a discussion of how important it is to identify and find resolve to potential risks to your assets in a multicultural and trans-jurisdictional environment. Finally, I will present what I find to be the best way to assess your company's risks, liabilities and integrity. Throughout the rest of this discussion, I will also highlight how putting forth a philosophy of transparency, accountability and cooperation in the global business market benefits you and your company's reputation. If you want to be viewed in a positive light, then you must act accordingly because reputations are burnished by concrete acts. In the past, business professionals and companies were able to strengthen themselves based on the quality of their products and services. Today, intangibles like ethics, morality and integrity have become the strongest assets in companies and are no longer irrelevant or hold a lesser value than tangible assets.

ASSET ALLOCATION: VALUING YOUR WORKFORCE

The 'lessons learned' from our recent experiences with fraud and corruption reveal that companies and individuals who have successfully preserved their reputations in the business community were able to limit their risks by properly allocating their tangible and intangible assets. In other words, they put all their eggs into one basket by focusing on their tangible assets. Assets can be tangible or intangible. Tangible assets refer to your company's physical assets such as its inventory, equipment, facilities and even investments while intangible assets refer to your company's workforce, brand and reputation. For the purpose of this discussion on risks, liabilities and integrity, more of the focus will be on intangible assets because *people* commit fraud and corruption and the effects of corruption damage your brand and reputation. Like tangible assets, risks are also associated with intangible assets. Unfortunately, these are often overlooked because they are unquantifiable. However, the value of leadership, employees, customer/clients, investors and other professionals associated with companies can be the most important asset class. Focusing on *people*, or human capital, as the most important asset class has led to the best decisions regarding mitigating risks. When intangible assets are valued in your company, and play a critical role in your long-term strategy, they positively affect your reputation, brand and the ability to retain qualified individuals. Companies that place a high value on their intangible assets like workforce, brand and reputation, are less liable to have systemic fraudulent and corrupt practices. These companies also minimize their risks because they are more likely to hire professionals who are specifically qualified to handle compliance and integrity issues. Hiring qualified professionals, and/or training existing professionals on these issues, turns out to be the optimal solution because consistent training and awareness of compliance invariably demonstrates a commitment to business ethics as well as fosters a culture that is conscientious about accountability. The next step is allocating these intangible assets efficiently.

Allocating your intangible assets, your workforce, is even more critical than ensuring your company hires the right professionals. In fact, hiring qualified professionals is, at times, secondary to how you allocate them and can be a key determinant of your company's readiness to handle fraud and corruption. The scandals that have shaken the business community did not lack qualified professionals. In fact, we can argue that those who committed fraud and corruption were sufficiently qualified and had knowledge of the system, at least enough to find loopholes and bypass existing compliance programs. On the other hand, mechanisms that would have prevented these scandals, such as proper allocation of human capital, reputational due diligence procedures, and whistle-blower programs, were ignored or did not exist. There was no transparency or accountability in the culture of the companies that were involved in these scandals; more importantly, the knowledge of their workforce was not properly allocated. In each case, it led to groupthink and there were no safeguards against it. There is not a standard solution to allocating your intangible assets because every company requires its unique solutions. However, because it is one of the most important decisions a company makes, finding the right way to allocate your asset is vital to conducting business with integrity.

Companies that fail to report fraud and corruption have also failed to properly allocate human capital and lacked diversity in their professional qualifications. That is, they were hired to directly focus on tangible, bottom line assets. While allocating your company's tangible assets is also important to minimizing your risks in a global market, a strong internal control system requires knowledge of local and global regulations. This is where your intangible assets, human capital, become significant. Qualified professionals will have knowledge of tolerated business practices in particular markets. Thus, investing in professionals with the skillsets required to conduct business in these markets will lessen your company's risk of fraud and corruption. For example, if your company is based in the United States and conducts business in Mexico, your company is still liable to United States securities laws, according to the FCPA. Thus, without knowing, your company may be at a higher risk because regulations may be more relaxed in Mexico, but your company is held to the same laws and regulations of the United States. This is an issue that has plagued several companies like Siemens AG and Wal-Mart, whereby they are held liable for the actions of their subsidiaries operating in emerging markets. As we know, the expansion of business into new and emerging markets has forced change upon the way business is conducted in developed markets as well. Clearly, companies conducting business in emerging markets have to focus on these potential risks. Because local customs in emerging markets may tolerate business dealings that are strictly forbidden elsewhere, the importance of qualified professionals that serve as barriers to fraud and corruption, specifically bribery, is augmented. Thus, a lack of integrity and culture of accountability may lead a company and/or its subsidiaries to conduct unacceptable business if value is not placed on intangible assets like human capital and reputation.

The value you place on asset allocation determines whether your business will be prepared to handle a crisis. The key is to know your customer by hiring and allocating your resources where they are most needed. For instance, companies like Siemens AG and Wal-Mart would be better served by assigning more qualified professionals to their subsidiaries that operate in emerging markets. Change is occurring at a faster pace as technologies allow for new and emerging markets to become part of the global landscape. As a response to these changes, relevant anti-fraud policies and professionals are needed. These are changes that require adaptive risk-reducing strategies focused on the knowledge that comes from human capital rather than reactive policies that can cause over-regulation. Placing value on your intangible assets, such as branding and reputation, and allocating your workforce allows companies to respond to conflicts as quickly as the market demands. It also helps them make better decisions to prevent or, at the very least, reduce risks. Companies that attempt to reduce their risks once a public relations crisis occurs usually do so to protect the brand rather than to fix what is wrong. This causes more damage to the company's reputation become it comes across as disingenuous and does nothing to restore the public's confidence.

The near collapse of the financial system set off calls for more effective regulation. Proponents of more effective regulation and risk-reducing strategies are right about the problematic state of the global business culture. There is a lack of transparency and regulators have yet to produce a solution that will hold specific fraudsters accountable for their actions rather than the entire company and/or industry. Under these circumstances, it is consistently easy to target the entire business community. This is why regulation can be counter-productive. It stifles competition and does not resolve the key problem. That is, companies have not placed enough value on their intangible assets and lack a strong culture of accountability because of it. To remain a leader in your industry, your company is required to focus on issues beyond its bottom line and its tangible assets. It also needs the ability to remain competitive without the restraints of over-regulation. Companies need to be fiscally responsible, cost-effective and are expected to make decisions based on their bottom lines. Yet, placing a greater value on your intangible assets will craft a stronger risk-reducing strategy that eliminates the need for more regulation.

A valued workforce will make enhance your brand, reputation and will not only make you a better competitor, but a more ethical one. Allocating and placing value on your intangible assets—workforce, branding and reputation—requires adequate and knowledgeable risk identification, evaluation and implementation of your compliance program. Your company's strongest assets, its leadership and workforce, must identify the opportunities for improvement. Furthermore, they should be able to suggest qualified solutions to these problems and implement them. The following is a review of risks that companies should prepare for when identifying and evaluating their risks.

UNDERSTANDING YOUR RISKS AND REPUTATION

The way we conduct business has changed. The reason behind these changes includes the way technology affects every part of our lives. Historically, this is expected. Societies evolve as new technologies are introduced. Technology has always affected the way we do business. However, globalization has intensely changed the way we do business because, save embargos and other political restrictions, we no longer have to consider distance when conducting business. New markets have been made available because of globalizing technologies like airliners, computer technologies, and, of course, the Internet. These technologies have also 'increased scrutiny from regulators and reduced customers' loyalty'.[4] New markets bring about new customers and, in turn, new risks. Because of globalization, we need to understand these new risks that new markets produce.

Technological improvements in communication and transportation systems have made every business process more complex. These changes have effectively convoluted risk identification, measurement and enforcement of solutions that minimize these risks. The simplest way to identify and measure risks is to categorize them. The following are the categories of risk that encompass the bulk of potential risks: reputational, operational, systemic, financial, legal and political risks. Every company has, or should have, professionals who study these risks, provide recommendations, and implement a system that produces solutions that effectively minimizes or eliminate risk. For the purpose of this discussion, I will focus on reputational risk because it is regarded as the most significant as well as most common risk in today's global marketplace. The tenacity of today's media, and their ability to act as an unofficial regulator, makes reputational risks the 'risk of risks'.[5] According to the Economic Intelligence Unit's Global Risk report, 'protecting a firm's reputation is the most important and difficult task facing

---

4   'Reputation: Risk of Risks. Economic Intelligence Unit's Global Risk Briefing'.
An Economic Intelligence Unit white paper sponsored by ACE, Cisco Systems, Deutsche Banks, IBM, and KPMG. *The Economist*. December 2005.
5   Ibid.

senior risk managers' and 'out of a choice of 13 categories of risk,' 84 per cent of 269 senior executives that manage risk claimed that 'risks to their company's reputation had increased significantly over the past five years'. This particular finding was concluded in 2005. Seven years later, reputational risk is even more important because of the technological changes that allow for faster and more information to be disseminated and accessed in a shorter time.

A singular and relatively trivial event can affect your company. However, events that can cause damage to a company's reputation are no longer singular in a globalized world. Thus, your response to these damages is critical. In a white paper released by the Economic Intelligence Unit's Global Risk report, six (6) key points were identified regarding reputational risks. These key points are valuable because they highlight the importance of a company's intangible assets in a globalized world and provide measureable results for risk identification, evaluation, and an overall assessment of a company's reputational risk. The six (6) key points are:

1. Reputation is a prized, and highly vulnerable corporate asset.
   – This preoccupation with reputation risk stems primarily for the fact that executives now see reputations as a major source of competitive advantage.
2. Companies struggle to categorize—let alone quantify—reputational risk.
   – Risk managers are divided on whether reputational risk is an issue in its own right or simply as consequence of other risks.
3. Compliance failures are the biggest source of reputational risk.
   – The biggest threat to reputation is seen to be a failure to comply with regulatory or legal obligations.
4. SMEs [small and medium-sized enterprises] lag behind on reputational risk.
   – Bigger companies undertake more reputational risk management activities.
5. The CEO is the principal guardian of corporate reputation.
   – The chief executive is pivotal in providing an ethical identity for their companies.
6. Good Communication is vital to protecting against—and repairing—reputational damage.
   – Reputation is ultimately about how your business is perceived by stakeholders including customers, investors, regulators, the media and the wider public.6

You have to expect your company to be imperfect and that losses will arise from errors and ineffective operations. Unpredictable mistakes are expected consequences of operating a business. But, reputational risks are preventative

---

6   Ibid.

and are 'a major source of competitive advantage'.[7] For instance, JPMorgan Chase's trading fiasco is an example of how a single event can instantly damage a company's strong reputation. In fact, JPMorgan Chase is one of the institutions that had the strongest reputation among stakeholders, investors, public and even regulators. JPMorgan Chase served as an example of ethical business conduct, especially after it was able to survive the financial meltdown of 2008. Yet, in less than 48 hours after learning about its $2 billion dollar trading loss, there were calls for CEO Jamie Dimon to resign from his position at the New York Federal Reserve Bank, there were calls for more regulation, and calls to overhaul the entire banking and financial services industry made headline news, once again. It is the same story with different actors. More importantly, Dimon, as the 'principal guardian' of JP Morgan Chase's reputation, acknowledged the 'terrible, egregious mistake' and vowed to investigate, as well as facilitate the US SEC's investigation, to determine whether rules were broken. In comparison to the lack of disclosure prior to 2008, the way Dimon has handled this event is a victory for transparency and accountability. It is also an indication of how important reputation has become in the global marketplace. JP Morgan Chase, and CEO Jamie Dimon, will likely overcome this trading loss because they already had a solid reputation.

How do you build a solid reputation? First and foremost, you identify the purpose and goals of your company. By identifying these goals, you will know what risks you will have to take to reach them. There is nothing wrong with taking risks. All companies take risks, some more responsibly than others. However, those who have committed fraud or corruption have perverted risk-taking. Second, exclusively focusing on risk-reducing measures will hurt your bottom line. The point is that if you only focus on risk-reducing measures and protecting the company from these liabilities, you will fail to reach goals. There is a difference between taking risks— winning or losing—and committing fraud. This is what causes the perception that business and integrity are oxymoronic. For instance, when a bank or financial institution takes a risk and makes a profit, there is no sounding of alarms. Yet, a risk followed by a loss generates massive attention in attack mode. The fact is that all risk management models are not failsafe; neither is regulation. If you are able to identify your risks and have success at taking risks, without crossing the boundaries of legality and integrity, you will gain a healthy and solid reputation. Stakeholders, investors and peers notice successful risk-taking and reward it. Finally, all companies take risks based on the possibility that an unfavourable event can happen as well as determining the potential cost of the event; the cost may be tangible (i.e., liquidity) or intangible (i.e., reputation). Your reputation is contingent on how you are able to successfully report on the risks that your company may encounter. The following section provides my integrity-building model to identifying, measuring, assessing and reporting on your risks.

---

7   Ibid.

ASSESSING YOUR RISKS AND BUILDING INTEGRITY

How your company deals with the risks of fraud and corruption speaks volumes about your integrity. The following is an overview of how your company can prepare for risk identification and build a reputation defined by integrity. Today, there's an incentive to be proactive about your reputation. Integrity relies on having a process that is transparent, builds a culture of accountability in your company, and places value on the balanced approach to regulation and self-regulation. While your company's goals have to be conform to the regulatory standards that are mandated by law, it also has to conform to global business ethics. We all have a clue of what is ethical and unethical business conduct, even if the law does not specifically address it. For instance, bribery, albeit unethical, is not necessarily illegal in many emerging markets and is sometimes an expected part of conducting business. For this purpose, your company has to take on the responsibility of doing business with integrity, even if it means losing a competitive advantage in markets lacking the necessary regulations. It may seem like a burden when other companies are not conducting business with integrity and have a competitive advantage because of it, but your reputation depends on it. Personally, I would rather be on the side of integrity if unethical behavior is discovered rather than have a competitive advantage that is packaged with unethical business conduct. The following is an overview of how you can assess your risks and build integrity within your company, regardless of the market and regulations you face.

Your risk management model has to reinforce self-policing and evaluate the circumstances that have led to fraud, corruption and other unethical behaviors in the past. Armed with the 'lessons learned' from previous misconduct, there are two measures involved in risk management: the external measures that includes rules and regulations, your key partners and suppliers, regulators, local communities, non-governmental organizations and awareness of how they operate and internal measures that includes corporate governance, standards and responsibilities, and your professionals. External measures are assessed by performing a reputational due diligence prior to engaging in business with potential associations.[8] The following focuses on mitigating your risks by identifying opportunities for improvement and making your risk mitigation activities more efficient. This involves establishing the measures of your risks and training your professionals to identify, analyze and report on them through a reassessment process (see Figure 6.1).

You have to first determine the framework of your risks. What are the risks present in your specific situation? This involves building a baseline for your risks and identifying the potential damages to your company's tangible and intangible assets. This also requires you to identify the risks involved by conducting business

---

8   Discussed in more detail in Chapter 7: Improving Integrity.

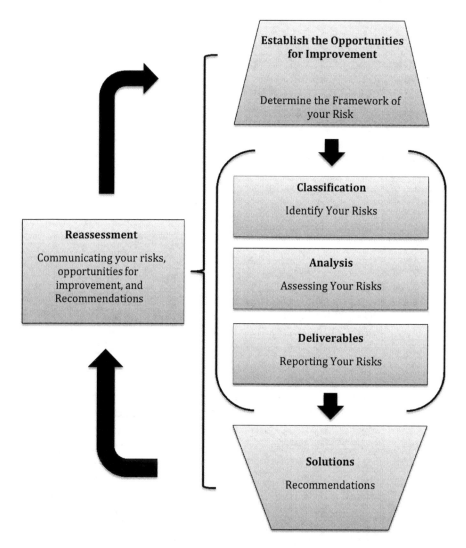

Figure 6.1   Measuring and assessing your risks

with key partners and suppliers, clients, and in emerging markets. This is resolved by upgrading due diligence procedures.

The next step, assessing these risks after you have classified them, involves making decisions based on whether some risks are acceptable or unacceptable. This is an important step that requires good leadership and qualified professionals that are able to make risk-taking or risk-reducing decisions. These assessments have to be realistic and the most cost-effective strategy should be selected because it is probably more productive for your company. The most vital step in your risk management model is its reassessment procedure. Reassessing your risks allows you to develop a more effective system because it provides updated recommendations that fortify it. The frequency of these reassessments can be determined based on internal and external measures. For instance, whenever a new regulation is introduced, an external measure, your risk management model needs to be reassessed accordingly. This allows your risk management model to develop in response to changes in the marketplace. Finally, reporting your assessments. It is important to provide solutions that can be implemented. This is the most important aspect to mitigating your risks. Proper reporting ensures your assessments are reliable and your company is building a culture of accountability and is capable of self-regulation. This leads to successful implementation of the changes required, based on your reassessments, to prevent fraud, unethical business conduct, and increase integrity in your company.

CONCLUSION

Fraud and corruption scandals on a massive scale have taught us that the regulatory and judicial controls set in place to try and govern the conduct of business are insufficient to do so on a global scale, and that while there are some encouraging signs of reform and improvements being made, it is essentially up to the company itself to create and cultivate an environment of integrity, preventing and mitigating risks before they occur without relying too heavily on external agencies to perform its role. In Chapters 2 and 3, I showed how corruption simultaneously causes developing and developed markets to suffer detrimental effects, especially reputational. Companies in each market are tasked with governing and holding themselves accountable for regulatory violations as well as violations of corporate policies in multicultural and trans-jurisdictional settings. These multicultural and trans-jurisdictional settings provide an example of the common disputes that arise when the inadequate application of a compliance program, one that is incapable of adapting to different cultural and legal frameworks affect the severity of fraud and corruption. The fact that, in a globalized world, multicultural and trans-jurisdictional issues keeping arising and for the most part are never resolved, reflects the failure of companies to create a robust compliance program that begins with self-regulation. That is, especially in a globalized world with multicultural and trans-jurisdictional frameworks, the change has to come through internal as well as external channels, because the former is more holistic and is a longer-term strategy. This chapter identified the risks as a result of fraud and corruption, specifically reputational risks, providing some concrete ideas of solutions. Every fraud and corruption case provides us with lessons that we can learned. However, the market is constantly evolving and you have to know how to adapt with it or your will be in trouble. Therefore, place value on, and properly allocating, your intangible assets prior to a crisis is recommended. The next chapter—Chapter 7: Improving Integrity—focuses on two of the most important aspects of any internal control system—due diligence and whistle-blower programs—which are essential to assessing your risks prior to conducting business. The purpose of performing a due diligence is to assess risks, expose the risks and minimize the risks by developing relevant recommendations, including terminating the transaction.

The next chapter emphasizes the importance of a reputational due diligence when assessing your risks because it does not only focus on reputation, trustworthiness and 'good standing' in the business community, but will also identify other risks and provides solutions for mitigating them to helps protect your tangible and intangible assets in the event of fraud and corruption. The fraud and corruption cases we discussed in previous chapters demonstrate why we need governmental and non-government international organizations and agencies that are suitable to combat fraud. However, the persistent increase of unethical behavior also demonstrates that it is more systemic and self-regulation and policing—such as changing the culture of accountability within your company—is proving to be a more effective way to combat unethical behavior.

CHAPTER SEVEN

IMPROVING INTEGRITY

Conducting business with integrity in a multicultural and diverse world is not simple. A company, its management and employees must comply with existing laws, rules and regulations while reinforcing a strong ethical culture in its everyday business activities. Not every compliance program can entirely predict and speak to every ethical situation it encounters while performing these everyday business activities. For companies, the greatest effort on remaining competitive in a global market. However, because our experiences with corruption are never far from view, the pursuit of ethical business behavior requires us to constantly find solutions to protect the integrity of our companies, employees, key partners and suppliers, clients and the overall integrity of the global market system. These solutions are found in the balance between 'soft power' and 'hard power' compliance tools in today's globalized business world. To have integrity, these two approaches to fighting fraud and corruption are essential. They allow you to create a better overall business strategy, particularly in the face of the changing nature of business priorities, the increasing importance of reputation as a main factor in decision-making, and the challenges of fulfilling your business objectives in an increasingly interdependent world.

After many years of experience investigating, reviewing and remediating ethical failures in companies, it is my experience that 'soft power' is much more effective at preventing as well as quickly detecting ethical and corruption problems than some of the more popular 'hard power' options. By 'soft power' I am referring to tone from the top, training and awareness initiatives, proper reputational due diligence on key stakeholders such as employees and vendors, open door whistleblowing policies and the creation of an environment where every stakeholder knows what kind of behavior is not tolerated and feels comfortable they can act against it if necessary without dire consequences to themselves. The 'hard power' tools such as audit, investigation, dismissal of employees and termination of contracts of vendors have their place in an overall holistic anti-corruption and business ethics system, but are usually too little too late if not combined with adequate 'soft power' initiatives (see Figure 7.1).

Soft Power Tools	Hard Power Tools

<ul><li>Tone from the top.</li><li>Training and awareness programs, including 'lessons learned' from case studies.</li><li>Reputational due diligence on employees and vendors.</li><li>Effective whistleblower program.</li><li>Culture of accountability.</li></ul>

<ul><li>Audits and compliance reviews.</li><li>Investigations and transparent actions to remedy violations.</li><li>Self-Reporting and cooperation with authorities related to any potential violations.</li></ul>

An effective business ethics program combines 'soft power' and 'hard power' tools:

- It engages employees and leadership by making your program interactive.
- It is preventative rather than reactive and after the fact.
- It is a long-term solution because it emphasizes the culture of your organization rather than a new policy.

Figure 7.1   Keys to an effective business ethics program

Solely utilizing 'hard power' tools to fight corruption has come under severe scrutiny, and the fact that the 'hard power' approach has been particularly criticized because it has failed to curtailed corruption. One the other hand, 'soft power' tools can be unsuccessful on their own because the requirements can be nebulous and do not always identify the causes and effects of corrupt behavior like 'hard power' tools do. Both approaches are useful to today's many global challenges and can aid in fighting corruption. A compliance system that mixes both equally or, at the very least, can place more focus on 'soft power' tools without necessarily having to compromise on the standard 'hard power' approach, is optimal and does not affect effectiveness. In fact, a balanced approach gives your compliance program a chance at being preventative, engaging and collaborative, and also provides a long-term solution. This is in contrast to many compliance programs that have been rather reactive, disengaging and lead to short-term solutions. More importantly, integrity requires that your leadership does not detach itself from and enforces a culture of accountability in your company.

To improve integrity in your company, and across the global market's landscapes, a 'zero tolerance' approach to corruption and accountability is key to building a good foundation. Company policies have to offer practical solutions about the expectations of employees, clarity about the dilemmas that corruption creates, and demonstrate how to apply existing resources to combat corruption. Corporate governance has the responsibility to outline these expectations, set a framework for accountability, and set a strong ethical example for management and employees. The experiences with the increase in fraud and corruption in the last 15 years illustrates the dangers of reacting with excessive policies, and possible over-regulation, while not considering the better solutions that a balance between 'soft power' and 'hard power' tools creates, including a stronger culture of accountability throughout your company.

Companies that are committed to conducting business with integrity are required to ensure their compliance programs have streamlined their monitoring and reporting responsibilities. Management teams that are charged with compliance matters for their companies must ensure these responsibilities are properly coordinated and each employee is trained to comply with all applicable legal requirements, rules and regulations and support corporate governance's goal. In our experiences with corruption on a global scale, finding ways to fix companies and improve integrity without impeding upon competitiveness begins with leadership. The tone from the top is just as important as training and awareness about a company's compliance programs' policies. Company leadership must collectively ensure that clients, key partners and suppliers, and other stakeholders, continue to build positive relationships and promote a reputation that relies on high ethical standards. Good leadership involves reshaping negative ideas about business as a result of our experiences with corruption that have led to resentments. The purpose of this book has been to offer insight into building integrity in business by applying the lessons learned from previous cases of fraud, bribery, and corruption. There is no sure-fire guide that can anticipate every dilemma that companies and markets may face. Yet, there are basic standards, rules and policies, events based on experience, as well as expectations that we can rely on to ensure the right decisions are made to prevent corruption, beginning with leadership and accountability.

The case studies in Chapter 4 highlighted the similarities and differences among cases of fraud, bribery and corruption around the world and how resolutions need to consistently evolve as globalization and technological advances change your company's business processes. These resolutions also continue to shape regulatory and corporate policies and provide clues about how integrity in business can exist in a globalized world. All forms of corruption have occurred globally, and while it has caused a point of contention in whether or not integrity in business can exist, there has also been enough evidence to suggest that many of the problems we have, and will continue to face as the market evolves, are indeed fixable. My belief is that the vacuity in public confidence in business as a result of recent cases of corruption, and the reputational damage corruption has caused, can be restored. To begin restoring public confidence and prove that integrity in business can exist, I examined past and current cases to demonstrate how transparency, self-policing, strengthening internal control systems, responsible legislation and media technologies, among other solutions, can facilitate the process of detection and prevention in a virtuous cycle of checks and balances. These solutions can thwart corruption before it develops into unrestrained and full-scale problems for shareholders, investors, companies, employees and public officials. Well thought out solutions also have a role in preventing swift and reactive decisions that shape the future of businesses. For every one of these spectacular cases of corruption and lapses in business ethics we have seen, there are dozens of good examples that never make it to press. What we have seen in the press has resulted in largely reactive efforts on the part of regulating agencies and corporate governance boards. Unfortunately, while reactive efforts lead to severe penalties and more regulation, and they appear to have done little to deter people from committing these acts in different ways.

In each case, lack of leadership and accountability, proper due diligence, transparency, and a lack of a variety of resources that provide awareness and training, especially whistle-blower programs, proved to place companies, employees, stakeholders and the market's reputation at a disadvantage once the corruption was exposed. This is an important trend. The severe consequences of corruption in the past 15 years have led me to address this trend while consulting several companies on their compliance systems. This has helped companies and their management teams build a compliance program that not only uniquely suits them, but also considers a variety of internal and external factors that are often overlooked. Performing your due diligence prior to engaging in any business transaction, ensuring there is organizational transparency, and having a variety of resources like a whistle-blower program to prevent corruption come from leadership and accountability, both important aspects of a robust internal control system. Leadership, accountability, and transparency as a result of solid due diligence processes and whistle-blower programs existed in successful companies prior to the increase in regulatory policies in the past 10 years.

It is not that these policies failed to detect and prevent corruption, but that a few corrupt individuals and companies chose to ignore them. This disregard for existing procedures created a perfect storm for failure, corruption, loss of revenue, and reputational damage across the business community. Unfortunately, the actions of a few have led to more regulation, which suppresses competitiveness and does nothing to improve reputational damage and change the ethical culture within companies. This is one of the reasons why corruption has been on the rise despite the increase in regulatory mandates. Internal changes, focused on leadership and accountability, will lead to improved integrity because a company's ethical culture relies on how it internally improves company-wide respect for its assets, products and services, mutually shared goals, accountability for behavior—whether positive or negative—and, knowledge of how each business transaction impacts employee, company and the business community's interests as a whole.

The media, more legislative mandates, self-policing and international organizations that fight corruption continue to foster better business relationships today. There are miscellaneous courses of action that have been used to fight corruption, but they have mostly focused on external solutions. This is partly due to not having enough trust in the market to correct itself; and, this sentiment is understandable and not without reason. But, more regulation is not the best course of action. Over-regulation can lead to a stagnant marketplace by reducing the ability to remain competitive. More regulation may be a good short-term response to corruption and does a lot to appease the public's perception of what government is doing to combat it but still fails to be the best course of action for the competitive marketplace. The pressure to produce short-term results can sideline the virtue of conducting business with integrity. Integrity is one of the most important corporate values and, while it may be seem to be difficult to put into practice without resorting to micro-management, the reality is that the success of any company, whatever the industry, needs a positive business reputation that centers on integrity.

Companies that have integrity have made sound ethical decisions at all levels and have consistently made good choices when dealing with their employees, business partners, investors and clients and are less likely to face corruption and/ or fraud claims. There are instances where individuals and companies have failed to understand these ethical boundaries despite having strong internal control systems; however, such situations are anomalies. Fortunately, there is a resolution: self-policing. Integrity relies on having a great internal control system where proper due diligence techniques and whistle-blower programs exists. Leadership must ensure their internal control systems hold these two programs as their most important assets. The difference between successful and failed companies is centered on due diligence and whistle-blower programs; and, also the difference between personal interests that can cross ethical boundaries and the interests of the company as a whole. It is not that good compliance programs did not exist, but that they have been ignored. Leadership, company-wide awareness and more training focused on your company's *existing* compliance program saves time, money, and does not obstruct your company's competitiveness in the global market.

How do we reach a solution that does not over-regulate the marketplace any further, but reduces corruption by a few individuals and companies? First, by strengthening existing compliance procedures. Second, by implementing programs and processes that focus and promote a culture of high ethical business standards. And, third, by collectively evaluating these programs and processes to ensure best practices as companies and markets evolve, and sharing them with the business community and the regulators as a whole. Upgrading your company's compliance system, improving access to information that will help your company's market position, and knowing your risks and liabilities prior to any business engagement are essential and less costly in the long run. More importantly, a focus on the ethical culture of your company in order to counteract fraudulent activities that can damage your company's reputation, and the business community as a whole, serves as an internal method of fraud prevention and conducting business with integrity.

The message here is, although external methods of ensuring integrity that exist in business are important, simply talking about and mandating integrity will not suffice. A company must find ways to incorporate the message of integrity into its culture and police itself in order to ensure integrity. Otherwise, we are left with uncompetitive companies due to over-regulation, damaged reputations, and a lack of confidence in the marketplace without any real solutions. Promoting and achieving integrity and a high ethical standard should be derived by internal means. While laws mandate more transparency, specifically in companies' accounting procedures, transparency should also be encouraged beyond what the law requires. Reputational due diligence and whistle-blower programs help reduce the possibility of having a few individuals cross these ethical boundaries.

Today's fast-paced global business setting requires flawless investigative techniques, precise analysis and a keen awareness of potentially damaging operational risks to you, your clients and company. There has to be a commitment to provide the highest level of services that produce professionalism at the highest ethical standards and sometimes at the utmost level of confidentiality. A company can no longer thrive in a global marketplace and hope to hide its flaws. A company's structure and its leadership directly determine its reputation because there is an immediate audience, the global business community. Compliance programs are forcing companies to meet requirements set by domestic and international law to deliver reports that prove integrity, especially financial services institutions where compliance reviews mandated by regulating agencies such as anti-money laundering requirements, 'know your customer', 'know your correspondent relationship' programs, and reputational due diligence services. Such programs are necessary to promote seamless business practices and reduce fraud. Yet, fulfilling the requirements placed on compliance programs is not the only reason companies are focused on preventing fraudulent activities. They are also focused on fulfilling these requirements because fraud itself is costly. In fact, one of the criticisms about regulatory mandates like the Foreign Corrupt Practices Act (FCPA) and Sarbanes–Oxley Act (SOX) is that meeting the requirements set forth by these new laws has been costly. Thus, companies' hands are tied because both corruption and regulatory mandates to prevent it are costly. The dilemma companies face today is remaining competitive and on task with their business dealings while making sure the requirements of these mandates are met.

The business of making money is still the reason companies exist. They must be able to deliver good products and services in a fair and free market system. While the idea that a more compliance-laden market produces honest business makes sense, too much compliance can cause obstacles for companies, especially those that do not have the resources to meet the requirements of these mandates. A stout due diligence process and whistle-blower programme are the most important and inexpensive forms of fraud prevention when compared to regulatory mandates and the costs of fraud. These two programs should serve as the front line of defence for every company's compliance program because they have the ability to filter out fraud before it becomes uncontrolled. There are countless examples of companies and/or individuals who attempt to connive and scheme their way through compliance programs and risk their reputations, as well as their associates' reputations, to reap immediate rewards. However, companies today that are more apt and willing to exercise due diligence beyond what the laws mandate remain successful and produce integrity at all levels.

The importance of performing operational, systemic, and reputational due diligence is more evident in a globalized world where companies are increasingly scrutinized by domestic and international regulatory organizations and the social media. Full-bodied due diligence procedures are not only able to solve internal problems, but makes it easier to resolve these problems on favorable terms and often lead a company to capitalize on business opportunities while mitigating risks at lower costs. By performing due diligence inquiries, companies will simultaneously have the satisfaction of being in full compliance, prevent them from entering into business with damaging associations, and protect their reputations. Knowing your associations does not only mitigate your company's risks, but also mitigates the risks of the global business community. As Chapter 6 shows, risks in a globalized world are operationally and systematically multilayered and interconnected. Understanding how these interconnections affect companies brings clarity to the idea that integrity, or fraud, in one company affects the entire global market. Most importantly, due diligence and whistle-blower programs provide accountability.

Accountability is a necessary part of corporate governance and is essential to having a stronger ethical business culture. It should permeate through your company, from new employees to senior management to potential associates who are themselves making the decision on whether or not to conduct business with your company. Accountability is about being committed to making decisions that show a fundamental respect for the company's vision, leadership, products and services, clients and industry. Furthermore, you must demand the same of your vendors and business partners because their actions impact your company's reputation too. The last decade's enforcement actions related to FCPA and the OECD anti-bribery provisions have amply demonstrated that 'outsourcing' your corruption problems to a vendor or third party is not acceptable and will be prosecuted. Accountability is a soft tool. It demands a company to improve its ethical culture through self-policing and lessen the implications that the hard tools of prevention cause from their financial and criminal penalties. Effective due diligence and whistle-blower programs provide companies with soft tools of prevention that are internal and hold companies and their employees accountable, but without inhibiting transparency mandated by regulatory agencies.

WHISTLE-BLOWER PROGRAM

A whistle-blower program enables employees to report company violations without fear of retaliation such as termination, reduction in wages, denial of benefits, non-promotion and/or any kind of negative retribution as a result of addressing a legitimate and verifiable action within a company. In fact, monetary compensation for legitimate claims is perfectly legal. Most whistle-blowers have both internal and external options (i.e., anonymous whistle-blower hotlines) that make it possible for them to report illegal activities without requiring them to give away their identities. These anonymous whistle-blower hotlines are meant to protect the individual from any type of retribution. The reality of retribution, however, does prevent some whistle-blower action. Accordingly, any compliance plan should focus on a whistle-blower initiative that encourages rather than discourages such action. Whistle-blower hotlines can be internal, meaning the fraudulent activity is anonymously reported via the company's compliance programme, investigated internally, and, if the claim is legitimate, the evidence is passed on to the appropriate authorities. Tips account for the highest percentage of fraud detection.[1] Therefore, instituting a proper whistle-blower program will significantly lower a company's risks and losses when combined with internal audits, fraud training and an efficient internal control system. The goal is not to create company snitches but to maintain an environment of compliance and ethical thinking within a corporate environment. Management and employees must be held responsible for reporting concerns and suspected ethical, legal, and/or regulatory violations. Those who commit violations and those who are aware of violations and fail to report them should be subjected to the full range of disciplinary actions.

---

1   *Report to the Nations on Occupation Fraud and Abuse: 2010 Global Fraud Study*, Association of Certified Fraud Examiners. 2010.

Even if a company has strong corporate governance policies, that include a whistle-blower program as an internal control measure to fight against fraud, the company will not always be able to control corrupt practices. External mechanisms are also needed to safeguard the integrity of your internal control system; thus allowing an external mechanism and outsourcing parts of your compliance program (i.e., anonymous hotline) adds another layer of protection. The success of whistle-blower programs is in their record of revealing operational and systemic problems within a business and/or industry and have, at times, led to reforms in laws and/or policies, potentially saving a company's investors significant amounts of money as well as their reputation. Unfortunately, no matter how much a company seeks to ensure it is compliance-friendly, has robust record-keeping policies, and conducts business with integrity, no company is immune to fraud and corruption. Every company is charged with the duty to understand how their organizational structure, staff members, vendors, suppliers and key partners' interests are aligned and proper in order to ensure that the company is not associated with individuals or business entities that are regarded as potential risks. Know Your Customer (KYC)[2] is the single-most important anti-corruption prevention strategy for your business. Without proper KYC policies and procedures, there are increased risks to associating your company's brand with unscrupulous individuals and/or businesses. The common denominator in fraud and corruption cases examined in Chapter 4 was the failure of individuals, businesses and even regulatory agencies to further scrutinize and demand basic information regarding those who they conducted business with prior to the engagement. In fact, just having someone ask the question 'Why?' might have even prevented some of the biggest problems. Having an enhanced due diligence process implemented would have saved investors, shareholders, the public and companies from becoming victims of fraud.

Whistle-blower programs are an essential part of your internal control system. They act as deterrents to corruption. However, employees must be aware about the importance of their role as a whistle-blower and the potential consequences of being misinformed and/or providing misinformation. Compliance programs are stronger if employees support its deterrents and are honest. While whistle-blower programs can assist compliance officers in discovering fraud, misinformation can and will place many people's lives and company reputations in jeopardy. Misinformation and abuse of whistle-blower programs can take away from the integrity of such programs, including the time, energy and cost spent investigating a whistle-blower's allegations. While companies are to be held accountable for

---

2   Know Your Customer (KYC) is a policy mandated under the Bank Secrecy Act (1970) and USA Patriot Act (2001) which focuses on customer identification programs (CIP) in financial institutions and other regulated companies to prevent financial fraud, identity theft, money laundering, and/or terrorist financing through an enhanced due diligence (EDD) system. KYC programmes are increasingly becoming a standard global business practice across all industries.

misinformation, so should whistle-blowers. Incorrectly reporting fraud can also be harmful to the company. Implementing a whistle-blower program, whether internal or external, requires commitment, the right tools, employee support, and proper supervision and training about the program.

Fraud and corruption do not exist as isolated incidents that can be resolved quickly and no individual or company is an island. Today, fraud and corruption by an individual, a group of individuals, and/or a company can have an enormous impact on the success and failure of other companies that are not only in their industry, but also in the global market. Failure to have a suitable compliance program with an appropriate whistle-blower program will bring about a multitude of negative consequences that are beyond damage to your bottom line. In addition, companies that do not create and conduct proper due diligence plans are highly susceptible to incidents of fraud, which in turn leads to unnecessary litigation and regulatory action, which ultimately causes damage to the company's image and bottom line because fraud also has an insidious effect on shareholder value. Creating an enhanced whistle-blower program will add to your company's worth in the investment sector as well.

Taking the extra steps to identify and manage your corporate affiliations, personal associations, obtain financial and/or legal background information via public civil/criminal/judicial records and/or social media websites using an endless list of available sources will reduce your company's chances of corruption and lessen the impact, in costs and reputation, of unethical decisions that can create widespread consequences, including a failed business. In today's global market, investors and fund managers are scrutinizing the integrity of companies' internal control systems to determine net value. A growing number of companies and individuals recognize the importance of conducting people with honest individuals and unblemished companies.

REPUTATIONAL DUE DILIGENCE

Reputational due diligence is the formal process of investigating individuals or companies for the purpose of providing impartial insight into their behavior and reputation by evaluating the potential risks of conducting business or associating yourself with the individuals or companies. Due diligence is recognized as the most effective tool to reducing risks and protecting your reputation when conduction any business in a globalized world. The simplest way to mitigate a risk is to eliminate those who would run that risk counter to your business culture in the first place.

Due diligence is one of the most important procedures you must do prior to engaging into any business contract. Most people define due diligence as a financial review of a company or individual's management, employees, key partners and suppliers, assets, contracts, legal issues, competition, etc. prior to engaging into business, but due diligence goes beyond numbers. The term due diligence first appeared as a procedure in the US Securities Act of 1933 under 'Disclosure Requirements'. Under this section, the Act made it unlawful for brokers-dealers to hide information from investors during securities acquisitions and contained the 'due diligence defense' which provided broker-dealers immunity from the law if information that was not disclosed in the process of their investigation was inadequate.

The problem with this disclosure was that it was limited; the law simply required 'issuers of asset-backed securities, at a minimum, to disclose asset-level or loan-level data, if such date are necessary for investors to independently perform due diligence'.[3] While the law mandated due diligence on securities acquisitions, investors were still permitted to decide on whether or not to continue with the acquisition. Therefore, based on the information resulting from the broker-dealers investigation, investors maintained the opportunity to define the level of risk they were willing to take. Over the course of time, due diligence has become applicable to investigations conducted during mergers and acquisitions transactions (M&A) and is increasingly becoming for applicable and required in other circumstances. More importantly, due diligence is the foundation of conducting business with integrity in today's multicultural and multi-jurisdictional global market. Companies have either fallen or experienced setbacks in their reputation and market value because they lacked strong due diligence procedures. Thus, because due diligence reveals the potential legal, financial, operational and reputational risks you and your company may face as a result of a transaction, it is your front line of defense in fraud prevention.

In practice, due diligence procedures differ by the type of company, the transactions and other external risks. In addition, as we have discussed in Chapter 2, emerging markets can potentially create additional risks that must be evaluated because, while developed markets have more standardized financial, tax, legal, and/or corporate procedures, emerging markets do not. In fact, both emerging and developed markets are constantly evolving so their forecasting risks, trends in emerging and developed markets, and collecting material information that is necessary to make sound decisions requires the methods and techniques of a proper due diligence to evolve as well. The central purpose of due diligence is to evaluate these risks and limit liabilities. This requires your investigation to consider as many aspects of the transaction as possible while analyzing past, present and future risks and liabilities. The task can be discouraging, but not impossible. Regardless of the type and purpose of the transaction, the following are key principles to keep in mind when performing your due diligence investigations.

---

3   United States Securities Act of 1933. Section 7: Information Required in Registration Statement.

When companies fail to police themselves, we get swift and expensive reactions from governmental agencies. These reactions cause external investigations, penalties, litigation and lead to more regulation and often have damaging consequences to industries while failing to curb corruption. Every industry has a regulatory agency that works with government to better monitor and enforce rules and filter out individuals and companies that go rogue. When companies follow the rules that govern their industry and police themselves properly by establishing a strong compliance program with an anti-corruption policy, have proper training, have a whistle-blower program, and perform their due diligence on each person and company it conducts business with, they avoid many of the consequences that have caused companies to fail. Unfortunately, industries and companies often fail to police themselves due to actual or perceived cost and this behavior runs the full gamut into fraud, corruption, and a chaotic internal compliance system where accountability is non-existent.

CONCLUSION

Integrity in companies tends to have a common theme, such as having an open platform for new ideas, a leadership that recognizes each idea as a potential opportunity and a method of assessing whether or not integrity exists in the company. The development of new ideas is the foundation of a successful company and good for business. Unfortunately, companies that do not have an open platform for new ideas or have a reputation for rejecting new ideas without fully exploring them are apt to have missed opportunities. If employees believe their leadership to be inaccessible or not care about fraud prevention, it will result in frustration and disgruntled employees. As we know, disgruntled employees may be dangerous to a company's reputation, especially if it relies on maintaining confidentiality agreements with employees because of the privileged nature of the work-product. Integrity in business requires a platform where ideas can be freely shared and decisions on whether to integrate these ideas are made only after careful review. Conversely, the commitment to provide an open platform for new ideas is not the sole responsibility of the company and its leadership. Employees also carry the responsibility of educating themselves with sufficient information about their leadership's ideas and how these ideas affect the company's goals, mission statement, reputation and other variables that are imperative to its overall initiatives. Finally, an important objective of any company should be to provide a service or product in a professional manner to its clients.

An open platform where ideas are freely shared and respected not only benefits your company, but it is also projects how the company conducts its business with clients. Companies that have a multidisciplinary staff and open platforms for ideas across cross-functional groups provide first-class products and services to clients. An open platform for ideas and a technically diversified staff produce certain values like accountability and integrity. These will help measure ethical conduct and address any cultural barriers that inhibit integrity from taking root in your company. An open platform for addressing compliance issues will help management discover the types of pressures that produce unethical behavior and define measurable roles and responsibilities to get desired results.

Examining each role and responsibility in your company's fight against corruption will lead you to a successful reputation. By conduction an internal due diligence of how your company operates, you will be protected by filtering out those leaders, employees, customers/clients, vendors and even contractors that function without the necessary integrity required to meet your compliance standards. To meet the necessary standards in a highly regulated globalized world, you must take a holistic approach to understanding your company, its assets, and each individual and company associated with your company. Beginning with the leadership of your company. Competent leadership is indispensable to any business. A competent leadership formulates and operationalizes new business policies and gauges the desires of their employees, customers/clients, vendors and their vendors' contractors. A competent leadership will also provide a unified view of business ethics. Companies that are successful and have longevity have good leadership, a strong ethical foundation, and evolve to meet new challenges.

As long as your company has these basic values in its ethical foundation and business culture, the right ethical solutions will exist, even if they're not always perfectly clear. The business world is complicated and constantly evolving. A company must adhere to the highest standards of conduct because it is the only way to maximize performance in today's evolving and competitive global marketplace. A culture of accountability throughout your company, along with competent leadership and an engaging compliance program, will reciprocate integrity. By having each person in your company inform one another and provide more than a mere perception of compliance, but have them actively engaged in the process, can potentially deter employees from corrupt business practices.

One of the challenges to ensuring integrity exists within the scope of your company's reputation is in how it responds to negative judgements against business integrity created by another's wrongdoings. Fraud, and other forms of corruption, by a few in the business community should not decide whether integrity exists in those companies who do 'follow the rules'. Yet, it does. Although every case of fraud and corruption is uniquely executed, the similarity is that each of their processes only remains unnoticed until that watershed moment when it becomes too difficult to conceal the crimes. Because all fraud and corruption has an expiration date, the benefit is that it will eventually be found, but a hindrance because we often have the tools and resources to understand and deter the processes, patterns and trends of fraud and corruption. Today, we view poor judgement and inappropriate activities as isolated incidents and continue to frame them as a result of an individual's, a group's, or one company's fraudulent schemes. Yet, because fraud is systemic and has shown to have patterns, or 'red flags', we need to strengthen our pre-existing internal control programs and discover meaningful ways to measure integrity to fit the context of doing business in a globalized world rather than relying on external regulatory mandates that thwart a companies need to remain competitive.

INDEX